Praise for *The Job You Were Born For*

"If you've ever wondered whether you can make ⸗ ⸗⸗⸗⸗⸗ ⸗⸗⸗⸗⸗⸗ ⸗ ⸗⸗⸗⸗⸗,
The Job You Were Born For is a must-read! Eileen has created a powerful guide for
aligning your work with your life mission, so you can live and work in joy. I know
it's possible because I've done it! Read this book, connect with what energizes you,
and become the person you were meant to be."

— **Ken Blanchard,** *New York Times* best-selling coauthor
of *The One Minute Manager*® and *Leading at a Higher Level*

"This book is a must for anyone who wants to live authentically and joyfully and
align themselves with their life's purpose. In a practical step-wise fashion, using real
life stories, Eileen explains how to identify and align with your natural talents and
abilities and live to your full potential."

— **Dr. Sheila Patel,** MD, Chief Medical Officer, Chopra Global

"A job hunt is more than just finding a job you desire—it's about finding the right
company and company culture to call your professional home. I firmly believe
looking for a job is one of the toughest jobs there is, which is why I commend
Eileen for providing such a terrific roadmap to assist anyone on their job search.
When you find your professional home and purpose in a company with strong
values, passion follows and makes work fun and meaningful."

— **Bill Stoller,** CEO, Express Employment Professionals

"This book, *exactly like Eileen,* is filled with inspiring real-life stories and practical,
actionable exercises and techniques. The book mirrors the absolute core of Eileen—
heart centered, caring, focused on you and your well-being—while strategically
guiding you with an expertise born out of decades of practical business experience.
I kept thinking, 'I wish I had this book 20 years ago, heck, even 10 years ago!'
Valuable for anyone, any age who yearns to discover and then align their life's
purpose on earth with their work."

— **LuAnn Nigara,** best-selling author and
host of #1-rated podcast *A Well-Designed Business*®

"An intuitive, divine, and practical approach to landing a job aligned with your
authentic self."

— **Shawna Allard,** award-winning author of *Knowing…the answers are within.*

"The book delivers inspired writing and pragmatic guidance. I am in awe of Eileen's unique capacity to draw from two seemingly polar opposite worlds. She flawlessly melds her extensive business consulting expertise with her dedication to plumbing our spiritual and intuitive nature. A must-read for those who want to align their work and life purpose."

— **Susan Fowler,** best-selling author of *Why Motivating People Doesn't Work…and What Does* and *Master Your Motivation*

"Millennials, Gen X, & Z would greatly benefit from the wisdom in this book. If they follow the steps in the roadmap and let their inner knowing guide them on their path, it will save them years of unhappiness, stress, and boredom from taking a job that is a means to an end. Everyone can work with harmonious passion."

— **Dr. Drea Zigarmi,** Founder, The Work Passion Company

"Eileen Hahn is tapping into the steps to success in life: awaken, examine, adjust, and thrive. Start with your beliefs, acknowledge the spiritual world's presence in your life, and get going on your journey to yourself. This book is a great guide for anyone who wants to make the best contribution to the world that they can. And why not? It's exactly what the world needs!"

— **Dr. Joseph Cooney, MD,** Founder, Berkshire Center for Whole Health

"While many of us contemplate bringing more joy and fulfillment to our work lives, we often struggle to do so. It's easy to fall into the trap of separating two important aspects of our selves, career and spiritual. Eileen's approach is unique and encourages us to consider the whole self. What comes through in every chapter of this marvelous book is that she is a true Earth Angel—guiding each of us to live and work in joy by stepping fully into our strengths, superpowers, and authentic selves. No matter where you are in your career and life journey, this book is a must-read."

— **Lisa Walters-Hoffert,** Co-founder and CFO, Daré Bioscience, Inc.

"Whether looking for growth at your current company or for an entirely new opportunity, Eileen's relatable stories combined with her logical, organic and intuitive approach will inspire you to examine and align your unique gifts to foster work and life fulfillment."

— **Rebecca Stolz,** Vice President for Continuous Improvement, Glenair

"Discover your life purpose and meld it with a passionate career filled with heart and wonder—highly recommended!"

— **Tim Ash,** best-selling author of *Unleash Your Primal Brain*

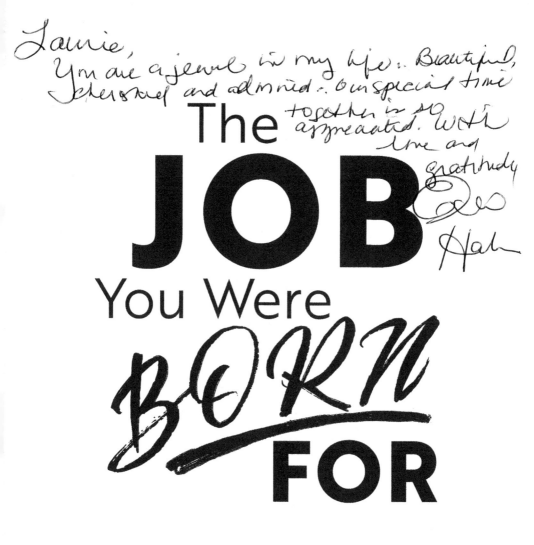

Laurie,
You are a jewel in my life... Beautiful, cherished and admired... Our special time together is so appreciated. With love and gratitude
Hahn

The JOB You Were BORN FOR

7 Steps to Align Your Work with Your Life Mission

EILEEN HAHN

HAHN HOUSE

HAHN HOUSE, INC.
SAN DIEGO

Published in the United States by: Hahn House, Inc. www.hahnhouse.com

ISBN 978-1-7377830-0-8 (print)
ISBN 978-1-7377830-1-5 (ebook)

Eileen Hahn
eileenbhahn.com
info@eileenbhahn.com

Production Management: Weaving Influence
Cover and Interior Design: Rachel Royer
Typesetting: Lori Weidert
Proofreading: Meredith Mix

*To my mother, Eileen Buehler, who throughout my life
encouraged me to live in joy and look within for answers.*

✱ ✱ ✱

*To my children, Trey and Gayla, who inspired me to write this book as they
embarked on their quests for jobs aligned with their life's missions.*

✱ ✱ ✱

*To my husband, Hal, who is my rock in life and provides
unwavering support on life's journey.*

✱ ✱ ✱

*In memory of my father, Warren Buehler, a pillar
of strength and encouragement.*

Contents

YOU'RE ON EARTH FOR A

*"Tell me, what is it you plan to do with
your one wild and precious life?"*
—**Mary Oliver**, Pulitzer Prize–winning poet

Consider this divine scene: You're in heaven and you're standing with God, side by side, looking down at the Earth. You admire the planet's beauty, but you also see its suffering. Together, you devise a plan. One especially for you.

Call it your mission.

Your mission's purpose? To ease the world's pain, while bringing its creatures peace and joy—at least in some small way.

To carry out your mission, God equips you with a mix of talents and skills that are unique. In other words, you have what you'll need to complete your mission, which will be knitted into your very soul.

After this beautiful scene, God sends you here to Earth, where you're born as a human baby.

At first, especially in your earliest years, you can't fully remember why you're here. But as you mature, you notice signs. *Major* signs.

Certain things, you discover, come to you easily. For instance, you may be physically strong or fast. Perhaps you're good at leading others. Maybe you can write well or play an instrument, or you're adept at math or science.

Why is that? Why those abilities and not others?

Along with those particular talents, there are certain environments and situations that call to you. That make you feel at home. For instance, you might be energized in speaking with others. Or, conversely, your favorite thing is to be alone. Whatever your inclination, it's a special part of your personality. It's who you are.

But, again, *why?* You don't quite know yet.

Gradually, however, the uncertainty starts to lift. Things grow clear.

As you make your way through life, these strengths, inclinations, and intuitions of yours start adding up. They don't seem accidental. They seem as if they're intentionally being guided by a firm and mighty hand.

Eventually, you remember. God sent you here on an important mission! What's more, you're endowed with talents and interests that make it easy for you to uncover that mission.

How do you know, though, when you're living "on mission"?

When you're doing what you should be doing, you're filled with a distinct sensation. You feel in flow. A wave of positive energy courses through your body and almost pushes its way outside your frame, into the air.

What exactly is happening in such moments? You're tapping into what I can best describe as a frequency of joy.

Whether you believe in God, the benevolent force of the universe, or the underlying interconnectedness of all beings, the principle is the same: We like doing particular things and are good at those things, because that's how we were built. Who we are and why we're drawn to specific phenomena and people is no accident. It's all a part of the divine plan that life has in store for us.

DID YOU GET THE MEMO?

Perhaps you've encountered people who love what they do and are making a special contribution to the world. People who exhibit an effortless joy and excellence in carrying out their work. In fact, their work inspires them to get up in the morning every single day with a spring in their step and a palpable sense of purpose.

Let's take a moment to imagine the life of a person whose sense of purpose is reflected in every moment of their day, especially their work life. They go to sleep feeling accomplished, peaceful, and satisfied; they wake up feeling absolutely rested and eager for the events of the day ahead: meetings with clients they love and whose lives they know they're impacting for the better; Zoom dates and social and professional engagements with colleagues and mentors they admire and who admire them in turn; and opportunities to put their hard-earned knowledge to use while simultaneously continuing to leverage their purpose to help as many people as they can.

Everyone this person comes across never fails to notice their cheerful demeanor. "What can I say?" the person laughs. "I love what I do, and I love my life." And they absolutely mean it, with every fiber of their being.

Sounds like a dream come true, right?

I want to paint a vivid picture of a completely different kind of person—someone who hasn't received the memo that they are here with a specific purpose.

They dread the day—from the moment the alarm goes off in the morning to the moment they step into their office (virtually or otherwise) and the onslaught of negative internal chatter begins. Unlike the first person, this one is not even close to thrilled at the prospect of waking up and going to work. It's merely a means to an end—and besides, they don't believe they have many other options. The job pays the bills and puts food on the table. Although these are what they have come to see as viable reasons for contentment, their dissatisfaction seems to grow by the hour. Every night, this person goes to bed feeling agitated by some minor mishap that occurred at work earlier that day; every morning, they wake up exhausted and uninspired as they contemplate the unpleasant things that might be in store for today: from bad traffic (or Internet!), to unsupportive colleagues, to a boss who thinks their efforts are never enough to—worst of all—a growing pit in their stomach accompanied by a sense of emptiness.

As this person hurriedly swallows down a bitter cup of coffee in the morning, they think, *I am so unfulfilled. There must be more to life than this! I just want to be happy and make a meaningful contribution. I want to love my job like other people do. How do I find my purpose and then that perfect job? Is such a thing possible?*

If you have ever been fortunate enough to experience the elation of the first person and that sense of being totally in love with your job—congratulations! If, however, you recognize some aspects of your own situation in the second person, take heart that you are not alone. And that there is a way out of the rat race and into the freedom of living your purpose.

Personally, I have experienced both types of jobs, and I have been in the shoes of both of the people I just described. You don't have to be unhappy and unfulfilled, but you need to be courageous enough to step away from the job that is making you miserable, so you can open yourself up to a job with joy and purpose. And that's why I'm here: to give you the nudge in the direction of your true and authentic calling!

BE THE PERSON YOU WERE MEANT TO BE

Chances are, you picked up this book in order to move yourself out of a job rut so that you, too, get to experience the power, creativity, joy, and wonder that are possible for everyone living in their purpose. The divine job strategies I lay out in this book come from over 25 years of management consulting work with companies like Anheuser-Busch, Ericsson Worldwide, General Motors, LEGOLAND, Pfizer, Sea World, San Diego Padres, H.G. Fenton Company, and others. While working with these companies, I have seen people excelling in the jobs they were born to do, and I have also used my expertise to help these companies hire more exceptional people. Overall, I have helped individuals and organizations thrive by teaching thousands of people the tenets that are part of my roadmap to finding the job they were born for. Now, I have put all aspects of that methodology into this step-by-step guide, so that you can uncover what you were born to do, locate that work, and land that job!

I have written *The Job You Were Born For* as a heartfelt guide that employs both my professional expertise and my lifelong path as a spiritual being, in order to help you uncover exactly what you were born to do—your special purpose—and use that awareness to land the job that is aligned and perfect for your authentic self.

There are three major existential questions all humans ask themselves at one point or other:

* Why was I born/why am I here?
* What am I supposed to do while I am here?
* Is it possible for me to have work that does more than pay the bills—work that is meaningful, purposeful, interesting, and enjoyable?

I'd love for you to stop what you're doing for a moment to answer those questions. What comes up for you? Although answers can sometimes feel few and far between, especially in this chaotic and constantly shifting period of our collective history, I'm here to assure you that they're well within reach! And I'm here to help you find them!

The Job You Were Born For is a love letter to anyone who has a secret (or not-so-secret) desire to have work feel like playtime; to do a job that fills them with joy; to come home at the end of the day feeling energized, excited, fulfilled!

Sound far-fetched? It's not. Some people love their job so much, they never want to retire. Why? Because they are doing what they were born—what they were *designed*—to do. (In fact, I know many people like this, and throughout this book, I'll share stories of how they got there.)

TIME TO LET GO OF THE EXCUSES

At this point, you might be asking: Why, though, isn't everyone doing what they were put on Earth to do?

The most common excuses sound reasonable, but they're based on faulty beliefs. People who unintentionally turn away from their divine mission say things like the following:

- ✳ "I have bills to pay. I can't worry about finding work I love."
- ✳ "I don't think the kind of work I'd love exists."
- ✳ "I'd rather play it safe doing boring work and end up with something, rather than give it my all to find work I love and perhaps end up with nothing."
- ✳ "I've blown my chance to find work I love, because I've made too many mistakes in life already."

Maybe these beliefs sound familiar to you. Beliefs like these cause people to ignore their natural gifts. Each belief works from the premise that all success looks the same. But that's not the case.

Each one of us is made to fulfill our destiny in vastly different ways. What success looks like for *you* might be outrageously different from what success looks like for *me*.

I personally could never work in the dental or medical fields. To be surrounded by blood and pain, day after day, would be unimaginable. But there are people who love that work. They were put here to do it! I know dental hygienists who feel at home in that environment. They don't cringe when they hear the sound of a drill or the crack of a crown. They show up to work with kindness and calm—qualities they're born with. Their efforts and cheerful demeanor come naturally.

Brain surgeons, too, feel comfortable, relaxed, and on mission in an operating room. They have no discomfort cutting into human flesh and bone, and seeing the delicate cerebral cortex exposed. While the work they do is literally life or death, the magnitude doesn't impede their performance. They have extraordinary focus and precision. It comes naturally.

This idea that you were put here to accomplish a certain type of work might be even clearer if we turn away from humans for a moment to look at the animal kingdom.

Our planet is populated with numerous creatures. Some walk, some crawl, some gallop. Others slither, swim, or fly. Some are drawn into action by the warmth of the Sun, while others hide until the Sun sets. Some are active throughout the change of seasons, while others recharge through a lengthy hibernation. Each creature finds a habitat that sustains it—a natural environment in which it can flourish.

Birds don't walk south for the winter. They fly.

Salmon don't jog along the river bottom. They swim.

Each animal does what it was equipped to do. Its species thrives because it follows its natural instinct. It stays, if you will, on mission.

The belief that we each have a specific purpose, possess unique talents, or have an explicit calling might sound like an idea plucked from modern self-help literature, but it's far older.

The ancient Greeks talked about the *daimon:* the spirit guide that lives inside a person, starting at birth. The Greeks believed you should put your daimon in charge of your life, letting it serve as your inner light during your life's journey. To the Greeks, if you tried to live someone else's life rather than follow the guidance of your daimon, you'd be miserable and squander your purpose, while denying others the fullness of your gifts and talents.

Your daimon, which I also refer to as your *Being* (with a capital B on purpose!), is your unique genius, which has its own spirit. Your Being has many talents and a mission that can both bring you joy and contribute to the greatest and highest good on this planet. When you tune into your *Being,* everything relaxes, gets easier, and becomes clear, and you can do extraordinary things in a highly impactful manner. All humans have an opportunity to tune into their Being and work in a job that utilizes their superpowers.

Much more recently, the concept of your unique mission and genius has come to prominence again through the work of Richard Bolles, author of the bestseller *What Color is Your Parachute?*

Bolles, who was a minister before becoming a premier coach to job hunters, said that people have three missions in life. The first two missions, you have in common with all of humanity: to know God and do what you can to make the world a better place every moment of every day.

The third mission, however, is uniquely yours. Bolles writes that it is to "exercise the talents that you particularly came to Earth to use—your greatest gifts, which you most delight to use, in the place(s) or settings that God has caused to appeal to you the most, and for the purposes that God most needs to have done in this world."

So, how do you find your mission? This book guides you to look within to your own Being. It provides a framework—methods, tools, pointers, and stories—to help you discover the work you were put on Earth to do. It tells you how to find and land a job using your intuition, or what I like to call your *inner I*. It points to how you can practically go out in the world and land that job you were born for. It combines an intuitive approach with a practical business perspective, so you can do the work you were designed to do. So you can work in joy and with purpose.

WHY THIS BOOK IS FOR YOU

Sometimes people question the practicality of my approach. They say to me: "Finding your mission? Working in joy? Who really does that?"

I tell them I have seen it many times over the past 25 years. What I have found is high performers in many organizations using their natural talents, in environments they enjoy, and feeling passionate about their work. They're clearly doing what they were born to do and are achieving exceptional results. They're "on mission."

It has been marvelous to see so many people over the years loving their jobs and performing at an exceptional level with tremendous results. Revenues increasing by hundreds of millions of dollars. Shareholder equity quadrupling with multi-billion-dollar increases. Employee engagement at unprecedented levels year after year. Team members smiling, laughing, high-fiving in the halls.

At the same time, I have met so many people who were not happy in their jobs. Perhaps they were even in the wrong career or company.

In studying thousands of people and assessing their unique pathways to success, the path to living in one's mission and joy became clear to me, and I wrote this book because I want to share it with you.

Before we go any further, I want to assuage any doubts or questions that may be arising for you and making you think, *Hmmm, is this book for me?*

If you believe that books about achieving your greatest dreams and finding joy in every moment are a luxury only afforded to those who have their basic needs (food, shelter, health, etc.) met, I want to assure you that this is not the case. No matter where you are in your life, socioeconomically or otherwise, you have a special mission that *The Job You Were Born For* can guide you toward. Granted, you may be in a place where you simply need to take whatever job you can find; even if this is the case, you always have the choice to move toward greater joy and opportunity. We all have the capacity to look within ourselves and honor who we are—the unique combination of gifts and talents, preferences and callings that were given to us from the moment of our birth—and to move in that direction. Sometimes these moves will look like baby steps, and other times they will be gigantic leaps. Wherever you are in your life, I am rooting for you and your ability to take the fork in the road that increases your access to joy and possibility.

Magic happens every day, and a major part of finding the job that will allow you to express the essence of your soul is remaining open to the opportunities that are all around us all the time. So often, we treat the journey of finding a dream job like a race to the finish line, but when we stop to smell the flowers, we come to recognize that it's not about *doing* something to get *somewhere*. It's about *being* who you are so you can discover the gifts that are already *here*.

There is no one-size-fits all when it comes to living a worthy and authentic life that makes you purposeful and happy. However, I have discovered from my work and encounters with people from all nationalities, vocations, and walks of life that the principles in this book are universally applicable. Whether you are a professional with a decades-long career looking to make a major shift, a single parent determined to care for your family and put food on the table, or a part-time college student who longs to someday secure a job that will allow you to bring your passions into the world—the methods in this book will enable you to slow down, look within, listen to what's calling you, be open to the help of Earth Angels (which I will discuss in greater depth later on), and use the practical advice included in this guide to lead you to a job that resonates with you at this time.

I say "at this time," because I do not believe there is simply one job, career, or profession you were born for. This might be true for some people, but each of us is multifaceted—and based on where we are and what we are dealing with in our lives, we may discover that our desires for our work and life purpose evolve significantly over time. Whatever the case, this book is always here as a steadfast and gentle anchor that will help you identify the ways you can meaningfully contribute to the world around you with greater joy and less worry.

While you will be reading a lot about the ways in which the universe is conspiring to help you on your path, I want to clear the assumption that *The Job You Were Born For* is all fun and games, lollipops, and unicorns! While I make a strong case for following the path of least resistance (more about that in Chapter 1), the journey of living joyfully and purposefully will include challenges, roadblocks, mountains to climb, and hurdles to jump; all of this will require courage and presence to navigate. The attitude you bring to these experiences is half the battle!

Most jobs also include tasks or elements that may not appear desirable upon first glance, but when you have selected a job that truly matches your mission, you will accept such tasks and elements with grace, and they will not detract from the overall sense of well-being and joy that you derive from the work. Whether you are helping to care for plants in a nursery, or developing new and exciting technologies for future generations, you'll find there is an energy and momentum in doing the work you were born for that propels you forward in times of difficulty. Such experiences will help you to grow and to share your hard-earned wisdom with others.

I also want to note that while the steps in this book have led many people I know to magnificent results, *The Job You Were Born For* is not meant to be a "magic pill" that will land you your dream job overnight. In fact, it's possible that the journey of this book will take you through a number of important and necessary discoveries before you can honestly say, "I'm exactly where I want to be!" The job that you were born for likely requires that you take steps in the direction of what is calling you. It may require building a foundation of knowledge and experience in an entry-level job, additional training or education, or several years of experience in a variety of jobs along your desired path. The diligence and perseverance to remain both focused on your desired path and open to the infinite possibilities for how it might manifest are necessary tools in your toolbox—so I encourage you to dig them out if you ever feel your spirits dipping and your energy flagging.

After I graduated college, I felt a strong desire to be a management consultant, own my business, set my own hours, and make a six-figure income. A seasoned consultant shared a tangible path to attain that goal that included starting in an entry-level job; getting promoted to supervisor, then manager; gaining years of experience and a thorough understanding of business; obtaining a master's degree; and having profit-and-loss responsibility. After all this, under the tutelage of an experienced consultant, I would finally be ready to live out my original vision. The extra labor and amount of time it took didn't deter me. In fact, each step and job along that journey felt aligned, purposeful, and joyful—which is always a sign that you're on the right path.

FOLLOW YOUR ROADMAP

If you are not living your mission, loving your job, and feeling aligned with your current life and work, *The Job You Were Born For* will show you how to do that. The clouds will part, and you will begin to see your talents and special gifts clearly. You will start to pay closer attention to what attracts and beckons you, and what physically and energetically feels right, comfortable, and at home. The path is easier than you think. It doesn't take a lot of time. It's about alert attention, listening, stillness, and cultivating the ability to tune into your inner I.

I outline seven steps as pointers to your mission. These are illustrated in the roadmap depicted below (which you can also download at www.thejobyouwere-bornfor.com).

Some people find comfort and support in having a roadmap to guide them. It helps them focus, provides direction, and keeps them on track. This roadmap will prove to be a trusty compass along your journey, but keep in mind that this is not a linear process that requires you to complete all the steps. It is possible to become clear on your mission at any time. In fact, the key is to let your intuition be your guide. You may find rest, comfort, and predictability in the roadmap, or you may realize a sense of freedom or ease in trusting your Being. Some things in this book will resonate, and you will feel drawn or inspired to do them. This is your journey, so ultimately, you are the guide.

This book is split up into the seven components of the roadmap. In Chapter 1, you'll begin by examining the beliefs—both supportive and detrimental—that contribute to your current job situation. You will also be offered tools to shift these beliefs so you can move toward what you truly desire. In Chapter 2, you'll awaken to your personal mission that you were born to fulfill by acknowledging your authentic self (including strengths and superpowers) and learning to follow the cues of your intuition, or inner I.

In Chapter 3, I encourage you to continue to connect to your inner I by listening to your innermost self in stillness—and opening up to answers and signs that will lead to what's calling you. In Chapter 4, I teach you how to be receptive to infinite possibilities and to continue to be guided by signs in the external world, and even by your own dreams and visions.

In Chapter 5, I shed light on the importance of communicating and connecting with Earth Angels, who can help you in the pursuit of your dreams. In Chapter 6, I encourage you to show up as your divine self and to access greater authenticity by engaging your values and interests rather than attempting to conform to a cookie-cutter version of what you believe a prospective employer wants. Finally, in both Chapter 7 and the Conclusion to this book, I end with an inspiring vision of what is possible when we absolutely know that God and the universe, however you wish to define this inexplicable force, is always on our side as long as we are open and receptive!

I believe the need for the path I've offered in this book arises from one essential truth: Everyone wants to know they matter. All people want to contribute to making the world a better and more harmonious place. We all deserve to unify and integrate our work, where we spend most hours of our waking life, with our spiritual life and deeper sense of purpose.

As you dive into *The Job You Were Born For* and respond to the reflection questions and exercises I pose in each chapter, rest assured that you will be led to astounding clarity around your interests, skills, and superpowers. Some things you will already have a deep knowing around—while other things will surprise and astound you.

You need not believe in any particular doctrine or philosophy in order to benefit from the teachings in my book, which have touched the minds and hearts of thousands of people from all walks of life. Just like them, you'll learn that it's possible to discover your mission, utilize your extraordinary gifts, and enjoy what you do every day. You can show up as yourself and perform your work in an exceptional manner. You can do what you were born and designed to do—while loving every moment of it and making a positive impact in the world! The more you listen to yourself and take action toward what draws you in and attracts you, the greater the likelihood that you will find and secure work that nurtures your soul and allows you to utilize your talents and gifts in an extraordinary and joyful manner. You have an opportunity to look inside yourself, to your very Being, and pull the unique essence of who you are into the world with joy and purpose.

Moreover, you'll continue to build fortitude, resilience, and faith that inner guidance is your trustiest compass when it comes to accessing authenticity and a deeper sense of purpose. The fundamental tools I offer will allow you to take bold, purposeful action, ask for answers, tune in, and trust that the experience of loving what you do every day at work is available to you—and perhaps closer at hand than you may have believed!

Chapter 1

EXAMINE
YOUR
Beliefs

> *"Examine what you believe to be impossible,
> and then change your beliefs."*
> —**Wayne Dyer**, best-selling author and motivational speaker

*T*he river's current was strong. It was, in fact, all but overpowering.

A man arrived with his canoe, dragged it into the river, and began paddling upstream—against the brutal current.

Soon, the man saw a monk on the riverbank walking in the same direction as he was paddling. Because of the current, though, the hard-paddling man and his canoe were moving at a crawl, so the walking monk was able to keep pace.

From the riverbank, the monk called: "Why not turn your canoe around? That way, you can paddle downstream. It'll be easier."

"Paddling downstream is what a lazy person would do," replied the man. "I'm not lazy."

"How long do you plan to paddle upstream?"

"Until I die!"

"Want to know a secret?" asked the monk. "In life, everything you want is downstream."

This is a popular Zen Buddhist parable that shares an important piece of wisdom that can inform us on the journey to finding our purpose: Often, finding joy in your work life is as simple as stopping your upstream paddle. Instead, you turn downstream and go with the flow.

You go with what is.

You go with your Being—who you already are.

You go with what you were put on this Earth to do.

Does going downstream mean everything will be absurdly easy and pleasant? Of course not! You'll still need to paddle. You'll still have challenges—like rocks, waterfalls, other canoes, and debris in the river—but navigating these challenges will help you grow.

At times, the river you find yourself on will seem huge and fast, with many tributaries from which to choose. You'll need to paddle with intent, resolve, and strength, so you can navigate toward the direction calling to you.

But remember this: No matter how demanding the current, another deep, supportive, intelligent current will encourage and compel you forward.

In a world habituated to struggle, going with the flow frees up your creativity, brilliance, and a sense of effortless ease.

As you head downstream, stay alert as you maintain a sharp focus and awareness. Look for guideposts and seek direction. Follow your intuition (your inner I, which we'll explore in more depth in Chapter 2) and let yourself be guided on the journey.

As you'll learn, even if you've been habituated to work hard at all costs, the power of flow is faster and easier, and it provides you with access to a greater capacity and more energy for joy and purpose!

Of course, I didn't always know about the power of flow. For years, nobody told me anything about the wisdom of seeking my purpose downstream. No one mentioned that my intuition could easily guide me to my mission. Instead, I received a different set of blueprints from my parents and society on my life journey in the form of commonly accepted beliefs that lock all of us into certain ways of doing and being in the world.

From the time you were born, you've received information from your environment, parents, family, friends, teachers, television, books, news, social media, and a variety of other sources, as well as from your own accumulated experiences. All of this has shaped your beliefs. Those beliefs have become your life blueprints.

A belief is a state of mind in which a person thinks something is true with or without empirical evidence to prove it with factual certainty. Some beliefs expand your horizons. Other beliefs can limit you.

To me, a limiting belief cuts you off from possibilities that might be lying in wait around the corner to help you move into your purpose. I know that wonderful things want to come into your life and help you on the path to fulfilling what you are here to do. But too often, we get in our own way. We unknowingly prevent these wonderful things—which can range from allies on our journey, to self-realization, to fabulous personal and professional opportunities—from making their way past the closed door of our limiting beliefs.

Of course, most of us have no clue that we're operating on the basis of limiting beliefs! We have simply been habituated to see our lives through a very narrow lens—a kind of tunnel vision that shuts us off from a clearer view of what we're perceiving. Think of how much one can miss when they are seeing life through such a lens!

A limiting belief can look like any of the following (notice in particular if you recognize any of these beliefs taking hold in your life right now):

* ✳ "I'm not qualified for the job I really want, so I'm not even going to think about it, much less apply."
* ✳ "It's too late to change careers, so I'm going to stay put and keep a stiff upper lip."
* ✳ "If it looks too good to be true, it probably is!"
* ✳ "I'm just going to get hurt or disappointed, so why even try?"
* ✳ "Being a leader means opening yourself up to criticism. That's way too scary, so I'm content to stay in my role."
* ✳ "What can I say? I'm just bad with money."

Such limiting beliefs hinder us from taking meaningful action in our lives, and they also create something known as change blindness, which actually works to filter out anything that doesn't match our picture of reality! That is, an amazing opportunity could fall right into your lap, but if you've been conditioned to be suspicious of good things happening to you, you won't even recognize the opportunity for what it is!

Our limiting beliefs trick us into believing that our picture of reality is correct, that "this is just the way it is," without stopping to question where such beliefs came from to begin with. This is how we often set ourselves up for continued experiences of difficulty and disappointment.

If you recognize limiting beliefs that are currently at work in your life, be compassionate with yourself. Most of our limiting beliefs are the result of our accumulated experiences, and while they may be frustrating to recognize, they very likely served to protect us at a certain time in our life—albeit as misguided attempts to help us maintain stability and predictability in a confusing and ever-changing world. Even if we don't like the results we're getting, our limiting beliefs are almost always a coping mechanism to keep us "safe." But all of us have the innate wisdom and tools to deal with the magic and mystery of life rather than chaining ourselves to beliefs that keep us small.

FINDING AN ALTERNATIVE TO "WORK HARD, PLAY HARD"

Many of the limiting beliefs about your mission and purpose probably come from your family or society—but most of the time, they don't actually sound like limiting beliefs. And sometimes, they don't even start out as limiting beliefs, but rather, as inspiring examples.

When I was growing up, a child of the 1960s and 1970s, the common beliefs shared by my family and friends often centered around our dreams and effort. For instance, my father would try to inspire me with the story of how he achieved his most cherished high-school goal.

"I had average athletic ability," he said, "with ordinary height and strength. But I wanted to make the high-school basketball team. And I didn't want to just make it. I wanted to be my school's best player. So I practiced more and worked harder than anyone. Every day, I went all out."

Eventually, my father's diligence paid off. He became a high school basketball star, received a full scholarship to Georgetown University, was named an All-American, made several Halls of Fame, and held Georgetown scoring records—despite a physical handicap in his hand and arm.

My father told me, "Don't let anything hold you back. You'll achieve your dreams if you work as hard as possible and never stop."

My father's example and his words were inspiring. To think—the sky's the limit! And if I wasn't getting what I wanted, all I had to do was work longer and harder.

Although the sentiment behind my father's words spoke to a deep and abiding wisdom about the human ability to move beyond perceived obstacles, the emphasis on "working hard" to achieve our dreams has also contributed to modern-day factors like workaholism, fear of slowing down, and a narrow focus on success at the cost of our own happiness. This kind of overly goal-oriented way of operating in the world can cause all kinds of problems, including chronic stress and poor health.

For me, the common phrases of my childhood also helped establish that ongoing nose-to-the-grindstone work ethic:

"When the going gets tough, the tough get going."

"Pull yourself up by your bootstraps."

"Dig deep and don't complain!"

"A winner never quits, and a quitter never wins."

"Never say die."

Phrases like these became the core beliefs of the time because they sounded like common sense. They came to guide my approach to life. In the words of Theodore Roosevelt: "Nothing in the world is worth having or worth doing unless it means effort, pain, difficulty…I have never in my life envied a human being who led an easy life. I have envied a great many people who led difficult lives and led them well."

Subsequently, the way I saw myself changed to suit these beliefs. I considered myself an underdog and a "scrapper." Maybe I wasn't the smartest or most talented one in the room, but I could work harder—and that exertion would get me far.

My greatest strength became my ability to "make things happen." I believed I could figure anything out and ultimately accomplish tasks at a high level. You could count on me 100% of the time. My enthusiasm and drive were exceptionally strong. I felt strength and power in knowing I'd never give up.

My life was full of pedal-to-the-metal activity. It was always go, go, go— whether I was working full time during the day, teaching classes at three major universities in the evenings, teaching Sunday school, or volunteering with a variety of organizations and causes. My personal mantra became "Work hard, play hard." Just saying it made me proud.

At the same time, there was some part of me that naturally gravitated to a completely different mindset. I felt encouraged, especially by my very supportive mother, to look within and discover my own interests, beyond what society told me I should be, do, or want. My spiritual path in life began at a tender young age, and I am certain that it impacted the way I saw myself and my life purpose. Despite the nudges to push myself to my very limits and to place a high value on working harder to become "better," I knew that I was in my excellence when I simply did what I enjoyed.

In my childhood, I was very outgoing, people-oriented, warm, friendly, open, communicative, and articulate. I emerged organically as a natural leader among my friends and classmates on school projects, leadership roles in student government, and volunteer roles. I enjoyed being a leader. It came naturally, fluidly, and easily to me.

Ultimately, I majored in counseling psychology in college because I had a strong interest in human potential and our power to access our depths to create better lives for ourselves. When I began working as a peer counselor at a middle school, I discovered that I walked away from my sessions with disturbed, withdrawn, depressed, and abused children feeling depleted and sad. Now, I could have gone on doing this work based on the mentality that working harder would enable me to help my clients and to feel more accomplished. But something told me to move in the direction that would help me access my inner energy and inner light.

I eventually went on to get a master's degree in organizational psychology—because I realized that helping people and organizations to operate with greater efficiency, effectiveness, joy, and success was something that energized me! It was fun and inspiring, and I was good at it! Today, top executives pay me to guide them to create actionable strategic plans that produce excellence; honor and impassion their employees; and achieve extraordinary high revenue, profit, and growth. Is it scary? Of course! But I'm up for the challenge because I love doing what I do, and I have the skills to do it.

One way to break out of limiting beliefs is to simply follow your intuition and to recognize when something feels good and aligned with your passions. This doesn't always mean that things will be *easy*, but simply that you are able to meet even the challenges and so-called roadblocks with a sense of joy and genuine curiosity. Rather than making you feel depleted, they make you feel more solid in your purpose. You trust that solutions will naturally arise, and you are willing to follow the path without knowing what lies on the other side.

Instead of following the "rules" (which include social conditioning and the beliefs that got handed down to you), you follow your gut—and in this way, you pave a new path to the future you want and the job you were made for!

THE EASE FACTOR

I still remember the day I awoke to the notion that maybe life didn't have to be hard all the time.

I was having lunch with two close friends, both highly accomplished businesswomen who loved life and cherished their work. While I knew a lot about certain parts of their lives, I knew nothing about how they started their careers and approached work.

Since my son had just graduated from college and, despite a prodigious effort, couldn't find a suitable job, I decided to ask them about their career journeys. Maybe I could pick up a tip that would help my son.

I was curious if my friends had worked as hard as I did, persevering through ups and downs until finally landing "the job" that launched their careers. Their answers caught me by surprise:

"I never looked for a job. Doors just opened."

"The job just came to me."

"Opportunities showed up in the strangest places."

I asked my friends if such workplace ease happened just once, or if their experiences reflected the entire trajectory of their careers. They both said that for 30 years, this was the way their entire careers had unfolded.

I was in disbelief.

They talked about how they were always open to and looked for opportunities and had a core belief that the right things would appear. "Look for the signs and don't be afraid to take risks," they said, "even if those risks are unconventional."

Sometimes they did things or took paths about which others expressed skepticism. Why did they get up and move to San Francisco...or New York City...or Costa Rica when they had promising jobs and business connections in their respective cities? These women seemed to have an intrinsic belief, a knowing, a trust that touched them to their very core.

It was similar to the trust I had in my ability to make anything happen through hard work. Yet something about their approach was different.

I wondered if I, too, could experiment with their path. Could I stop working so hard, expending so much time and energy—and *still* make things happen? Would the results be the same? Could they be even better?

I left lunch understanding I needed to explore this concept. I decided to ask others I knew in my personal and professional life about their journeys: people who enjoyed their jobs, used their talents, and prospered. I was surprised by how many shared the belief that life can just open up for you if you let it, encourage it, and look for signs.

One person had a name for it: the ease factor.

She said, "Part of what I've done my whole life was look for paths that beckoned me, attracted me, and were easy. If I felt I was pushing or pulling too much, or if things got really hard, I'd stop. I'd get quiet, close my eyes, and look inside for guidance. I'd ask myself if I was going in the right direction. Or was there a different direction I hadn't thought about before? Or if I were butting heads with some obstacle, I'd ask myself if there was a way to meet that obstacle and move with it or around it."

When she said this, it made me realize that even when we follow the path of flow and move with ease, we are always actively making choices about the tributaries we take. It made me recognize that this actually already applied to my life!

When I reflected on other aspects of my life outside of work, such as making friends, meeting my spouse, and traveling internationally, I recognized that they all just flowed. They were never hard. I never had to work at them or grit my teeth.

I also thought of my experiences with work, which led me to identify ways I actually went around obstacles rather than just powering through them. When I first graduated from college, I searched for human resources assistant jobs, but to my disappointment, every job wanted one to two years of prior experience—and I had none (a phenomenon that most college grads will recognize). Over the course of my career, I have realized that this perceived "obstacle" doesn't have to stop us—or make us give up that easily. I've learned it's a good idea to apply for the job even if you don't think you're qualified, and to also begin talking to other people who work in that field to see what their advice might be.

When it comes down to it, where there's a passion, there's a way.

I secured my first job out of college at an employment agency, placing people in jobs and learning HR work simultaneously. For this reason, I jumped over the "obstacle" of not being able to get an HR assistant job due to my lack of experience. I went from being an account executive at the employment agency to a corporate training director—a job that most people wouldn't be able to get unless they already had training experience—to an HR director within a short period of time.

So, instead of going the traditional route of "working my way up" to the HR director role from the assistant position, I took an unlikely path that actually made achieving my goal faster and easier! By taking this path, I continued to follow the signs and move toward what felt natural and enjoyable—and I managed to gracefully navigate a combination of roadblocks and challenges by maintaining an attitude of flexibility and openness.

And ideally, that is what you will also do as you step into your mission and find the job you were born to do.

All of the examples I have mentioned can apply to your own job search. All that's required is the willingness to understand how your beliefs may be creating a roadmap for your job search. Is this roadmap clear, legible, and filled with easeful trajectories? Or is it unnecessarily complicated, with contradictory routes and unexpected dead ends?

Make no mistake: Your beliefs *are* a roadmap. They will determine the remainder of your journey, so it is well worth your time to examine them and see if any need updates.

Exercise: Recognize and Change Your Beliefs about Your Job Search

Be open to the possibility that life, your mission, and your job search can unfold simply. Things don't have to be hard. It needn't be a battle, waged or won. There are road signs, hints, and callings galore. You just need to stop for a gentle moment, close your eyes, look inside, and listen. Then, open your eyes to see the signs and clues. Hear the voice, trust your being, walk the path, and don't be afraid to take risks.

Once beliefs are formed, we tend to look for ways to validate them rather than looking at options, perspectives, and experiences that might challenge them. It's important to be open to new beliefs, whether we choose to adopt them or not.

A wonderful thing about beliefs is that you can change them at any time. Ask yourself:

* What beliefs do I have about work and jobs?
* Is work a means to an end, or is it an opportunity to have fun and use my talents?
* In what ways are my beliefs limiting me?
* In what ways are my beliefs helping or serving me?
* Am I ready to try something else?
* Am I open to the infinite possibilities of the universe?

THE POWER OF COURAGE

As we've explored, examining beliefs is the first step to purposefully living out your one wild and precious life and doing work you were born to do. It is important to acknowledge your thoughts and beliefs so you can now open your eyes to who you really are and what you were designed to do. The next step is to see yourself and your magnificence—to identify the talents and gifts bestowed upon you to carry out your mission.

In order to access your fullest and truest Being, you must develop the courage to look at yourself clearly. Courage is what helps us open our hearts to new possibilities and move beyond limiting beliefs. When we act with courage, it becomes a self-fulfilling prophecy that allows us to feel validated when we stretch outside of our comfort zone. It becomes a trusted compass because we see and feel the results of doing and seeing things differently.

At 56 years old, I've summoned courage so many times and have seen how it worked out, and it continues to give me the confidence and perspective to keep going—to keep taking that leap of faith.

As an example of a leap I took, many years ago I moved from the East Coast to the West Coast to go to college and find a job. I'd already taken the leap of changing my focus from counseling psychology to organizational psychology, and now I was ready to find the job I was born for. The first job I took (which I mentioned earlier in this chapter), I worked on $1,000 a month, draw vs. commission, right out of college. I ended up getting lucrative consulting work and obtaining my master's degree. Each leap of faith led to another leap of faith and has helped me to guide others into taking their own magnificent leaps!

This book is here to help you do the same. I want you to consider all the leaps you've already taken—and the limiting beliefs you've already moved beyond. It's likely you've experienced countless courageous moments of your own, otherwise you wouldn't be reading this right now. It's so important to acknowledge the incredible work you've already done so you are armed with the confidence and encouragement to keep leaping—until it becomes second nature. So even when you come face-to-face with old, familiar questions like, "Who am I to think I can do this big and important thing with my life?" you'll have what it takes to keep showing up. You'll be able to allow your mission to beautifully unfold before you so that you can fully step into your calling.

Chapter 2

KNOW YOURSELF, KNOW YOUR *Magnificence*

> *"Knowing yourself is the beginning of all wisdom."*
> —**Aristotle**, ancient Greek philosopher

"Know thyself."

These are the immortal words inscribed over the door to the ancient temple of the Oracle of Apollo at Delphi in Greece. People from all over the world come to this place in order to pay homage to its sacred mystery. Delphi also happens to be home to a list of 147 maxims, or commandments, on living a good and morally virtuous life. The commandments were thought to have been put together by the Seven Sages, a group of distinguished Greek philosophers and lawmakers. But of all 147 commandments, "Know thyself" is the most familiar and fundamental.

What does it truly mean to "know thyself"? What exactly is it that we need to know? What even *is* the self? The poet Rumi asked, "When will I ever see that Am that I Am?" Countless poets, students, and everyday dreamers have ruminated on such questions since time immemorial.

It is all too easy to fall into the game of comparison, judging ourselves on the basis of arbitrary criteria that deem some people's talents "valuable" and others "useless." But one of the major gifts of self-knowledge is that we are able to claim our true Being and our authentic potential. As we become more aware of who we are, through awareness of our thoughts and beliefs (which we discussed in Chapter 1) and awareness of our bodies (which we'll go into in more detail in this chapter), we can finally learn to celebrate ourselves on our own terms and discover the work we were born to do.

St. Therese of Lisieux once said, "If every tiny flower wanted to be a rose, spring would lose its loveliness."

It is not through comparison that we come to achieve greatness; it is only in fully loving and accepting our unique contribution to the intricate tapestry of life that we finally recognize our own significance. In this way, we can learn to co-create with the universe so that we are going with the flow of life and welcoming an experience of ease and harmony.

True self-knowledge consists of understanding who we are from the inside out: where we have come from, where we are going, and what our unique purpose on this planet is. When we achieve this, we truly come to know our divine essence. Remember, your unique purpose has been granted to you by a source that longs for you to uncover the hidden sparks of divinity that live within. This chapter covers the power of harnessing the deepest knowledge of who you are in order to ignite your life with the fire of your passion and purpose. The good news is that you don't have to make a pilgrimage to an ancient sacred site in order to dance with the mystery of your deepest self—it's available to you right here, right now.

THE FOUR KEYS TO SELF-KNOWLEDGE

Picture this: A group of small children, between the ages of four and six, enter a giant playroom together. Lining the walls are a colorful variety of activity areas and play stations. One area is full of crayons, markers, paints, paper, yarn, glitter, glue, and a plethora of other art supplies all laid out and ready to be put to use. Another station has puzzles, Rubik's cubes, blocks, and a Jumbo Jenga setup. Across the way is an enormous dollhouse full of dolls, miniature furniture, closets of doll clothes, and realistically imagined scenarios that the dolls might find themselves in. Yet another station includes balls, bats, basketball hoops, and other sporting items. As far as the eye can see, there are tools and activities that appeal to an assortment of interests and talents: from musical instruments to books, remote-control cars to chemistry sets, materials to build a treehouse to Karaoke machines that let aspiring singers belt out a tune.

The children immediately bolt toward what draws them, without having to think for a second about what they will choose. The room is filled with the sounds of laughter, delighted shrieks, and animated conversation as the children immediately lose themselves in hours of play.

At some point, a loud bell rings and a procession of teachers, parents, and other adults come into the room, clapping their hands and attempting to summon order in this space of creative chaos. The adults begin to relay a variety of messages all at once:

"You need to focus on the basics: reading, writing, and arithmetic."

"You have to be good at everything you do—nothing less than straight A's."

"You can't focus on what you love—that's just impractical and will never get you a good job that pays well!"

"Forget about your passion. Making money and being respected by others is the most important thing."

"Life isn't about being happy—it's about doing what's responsible so you can always afford to put food on the table."

The joyful noise turns to silence; the happy faces and easeful confidence become downcast eyes and slumped shoulders. The children slowly file out of the magical playroom and into the lives that await them.

The scenario I described is a metaphor for what so many of us experience when our early childlike wonder and natural gifts are squashed by society's ideas about who we should be in order to become "successful," responsible, well-adjusted adults. Unfortunately, many of us unquestioningly fall into lock step with these ideas and lose sight of that spark of inspiration that lies buried within us. We lose sight of our precious time, our precious joy, our precious passion. We end up living on autopilot and continuing to hit the snooze button on the alarm clock as we head into our days and our lives, numbed to that deeper sense of connection to ourselves and what truly moves us.

How does the prospect of living this way for the rest of your life sound to you? Pretty dreadful, right? Your potential is so much bigger than that. You know you are here to fulfill a much grander purpose than waking up each morning and living out the same mind-numbing routine of doing what you are "supposed" to do.

In order to reconnect to your Being and your mission, it is crucial that you answer the following questions, which I like to refer to as the **four keys to self-knowledge** because of their magical ability to unlock our latent gifts and talents:

* ✳ What mysteriously attracts you?
* ✳ What are you naturally good at?
* ✳ What do you genuinely enjoy doing?
* ✳ What feels good or right in your body—that is, it gets you excited, gives you energy, and infuses you with a sense of goodness, exuberance, or well-being?

Every single person has a unique combination of answers that corresponds to their specific personality, style, and temperament—and no one path is better or worse than another. What matters most is that you feel aligned with whatever it is you are doing and whoever it is you are Being in any given moment.

For many of us who might not have been taught to consider our feelings, thoughts, and opinions, or who were encouraged to suppress them in order to fit in and be accepted, digging into our personal truth might feel a little like being an archaeologist on a dig. But I want to assure you that even if you think you don't know the answers, on some level, you *do*. So, treat the process of excavation like an adventure that is sure to unearth some exciting surprises and familiar mementos. Be open to what you discover.

To find the job you were born for, you need to better understand yourself and be clear about your strengths, skills, and interests. Taking time to self-reflect is an important aspect of ensuring that we are not simply living on autopilot, and that we are accessing the joyful, wonder-filled child that lives within us—that child who is effortlessly connected to what truly makes us light up and fills us with purpose.

To this end, self-knowledge is not simply an intellectual exercise but one that engages all aspects of our soul. When we are fully expressing ourselves through joyful activity, we are engaged in self-knowledge of the highest order. So, remember to use the four questions above as keys that will always bring you back to yourself and provide you with the clarity and direction you need in order to find the job you were born for!

Exercise: What Do You Enjoy?

The following questions will get you thinking differently about your interests, talents, and abilities. You'll also be referring to them as you move through the remainder of this chapter.

Take time to stop what you are doing and offer yourself the gift of going inward. Sit with yourself and allow the answers to the following questions to effortlessly bubble out of you. Often, your first thought is your best thought. Don't try too hard or stress over answering the questions "correctly"—the answers already live within you.

* What activities did you enjoy doing as a child?
* What do you enjoy doing today?
* What do you get excited about doing?
* What energizes you when you do it?
* What activities strengthen you?
* Is there something you do that absorbs your attention so much that you don't notice time passing?
* When are you sharp, clear, focused, and in the moment?
* What could you do all day long?
* What is fun for you and feels practically like playtime?
* What lights you up when you talk about or do it?
* What puts a smile on your face?
* What activity enlivens you, or propels you to be your best self?
* What is so noticeably central to who you are that those closest to you—parents, spouses, and friends—know what it is and can see it in you?

IDENTIFY YOUR STRENGTHS

Another important part of knowing yourself is owning what you're good at. By identifying your natural strengths, you'll have a clue as to which missions and jobs best align with your gifts. This process of determining your strengths provides insight into the mix of talents and strengths bestowed upon you, and it helps you figure out how they might apply in the world.

Bridging your abilities to the skills employers want for specific jobs will help you on this journey. When employers are looking to fill a position, they identify the technical skills and performance skills needed so they can target people with those skills. Employers design selection and interview processes to determine whether an applicant has those skills. Understanding your strengths in relation to what employers are looking for will make it easier for you to navigate the employment and selection process to find and land a job that is aligned with your mission—a job in which you will feel at home.

Let's take time now to translate your strengths to what employers are looking for: technical and performance skills.

A technical skill is the ability to carry out a task that requires technical knowledge or training to perform and master the task. For example, if you've never learned how to create an Excel spreadsheet, you wouldn't be able to sit down at a computer and create one right now. If you were never trained to operate a forklift, you couldn't just jump into the cab of one and drive it with expertise.

Technical skills can relate to mechanical operations (e.g., installing an HVAC system), information technology (e.g., programming or using certain types of software), mathematical work (e.g., accounting, modeling, forecasting), or scientific tasks (e.g., pipetting, transfecting cells, interpreting histograms). They can also relate to other types of expertise, such as how to conduct an effective, legally defensible interview, or how to lead and facilitate strategic-planning meetings. (Please see Appendix 1 for examples of technical skills.)

Performance skills are the manner or way in which you perform tasks. People have a spectrum of efficacy in these skills. For example, some people have a high attention to detail, while others have a low attention to detail and a greater investment in the big picture. Some people are highly proactive, and some are more reactive and good at taking direction. Some people work well managing multiple priorities, and some are less effective at it but tend to have laser focus and impeccable attention when they are doing one task at a time. (Please see Appendix 2 for examples of performance skills.)

If you have difficulty identifying your skills, consider asking a handful of trusted, respected colleagues and mentors for their estimation of what makes you shine and where you perform well. One note of caution: As much as you might respect the feedback of others, it's important that you take time to examine yourself before receiving advice and input from others. Be clear about who you are before you ask someone else for their opinion.

CLAIM YOUR SUPERPOWERS

Every single person has a unique genius, a divine gift, that is all their own. And this genius comes with a variety of superpowers that enable it to be expressed in the world. A superpower is something you do easily, naturally, and exceptionally well. You need this power to carry out your mission. Beyond simply being a skill that you are able to perform in the world, your superpower is something you enjoy doing. Time passes quickly while you do it, and the activity energizes and strengthens you.

When we are displaying our superpower, we are expressing the kind of vitality that fills us with a noticeable radiance. Unfortunately, we don't often recognize our superpowers as strengths, because they come to us so easily and naturally. Their ease obscures their significance.

While you may have many "powers"—including the strengths and talents you identified under your technical and performance skills—your superpowers tie the whole package together. Knowing your superpowers makes it easier to identify your mission. And ultimately, you need your superpowers to carry out your mission.

I've conducted hundreds of 360-degree leadership feedback sessions, with leaders ranging from supervisors to CEOs. When people rave about a particular leader's abilities in a specific area, I ask that leader, "What do you do that makes you so extraordinary?" Invariably, their answer sounds something like this: "I don't know. I'm just being me."

For one 360-degree session, I was working with a 25-year career professional, Bill, the dean of a major university. Some of the comments about him included: "Bill shows compassion and care in everything he does"; "He takes on challenges without pause"; "If his first approach doesn't work, he is open to alternatives"; and "Bill doesn't seem to back away at any point from a tough situation or adversity. If anything, he leans into it."

In general, the comments painted him as a man who calmly and directly approached conflicts and could fluidly navigate a difficult situation until there was resolution. I asked Bill whether he saw these comments as true.

He said, "Yes. But doing that stuff isn't something I think about much. It comes naturally." Then he laughed. "It's funny. When I graduated college decades ago, I'd never have thought I'd become a dean of students. But for some reason, I'm comfortable doing it and enjoy it."

In Bill's case, he found it funny that he ended up in his current role, as it was something he'd never considered when he was a student himself. Yet his natural talents—his superpowers—led him to this post because they perfectly aligned with the job's required skill set. And they were visible to everyone around him. The match resulted in a job at which he excelled, was recognized for, and most importantly, that he loved.

Sometimes superpowers surface at a tender age. I remember meeting a young girl who scored 100% on all her tests in history, science, and vocabulary. When I asked her how she did it, she said, "It's easy. I have a photographic memory. I see something once and just call back the memory."

As this girl continued through school, she looked to her inner self for guidance more and more. When she read a chapter in a book, she would look at each page as if she were taking a picture of it in her mind. She would notice the graphs, charts, pictures, and words on a page in a way that most people did not. If a word was bolded, enlarged, or pulled out, she experienced it in a heightened manner. She was mindful of what was on the page and that she would be coming back to that page when taking a test.

She studied for tests with the confidence that if she reviewed the information, she would simply be able to look within and recall it. And she did. Years later, when she attended college, she had to write a ten-page research paper, so she decided to see if the paper would come forth from within her, just as the right facts, figures, and stories had appeared in her mind during tests. And it did. In only a few hours, she wrote the entire paper from an internally guided place. It received an A. This experience, she said, encouraged her to be open to the knowledge and power inside her.

After that experience, she incorporated the same practice in approaching all her papers and assignments, and she continued getting A's. This young woman's capability to pull her knowledge from within—almost as if it were stored in a vault in her body that could be accessed at will—is one of her superpowers. I will explain this concept of looking within for answers in further detail in Chapter 3.

A photographic memory may not be your superpower. It isn't mine! The good news is that the list of superpowers is endless, wide, and varied, and somewhere on that list are yours!

For some people, a superpower can be the ease of public speaking, throwing an elegant dinner party for a hundred people, scrapbooking, fundraising, arranging flowers, interior decorating, creating music, painting, relating to people of all ages or a specific age or demographic, being an empathetic listener, creating complex spreadsheets, forecasting, analyzing and synthesizing data, etc. The list goes on and on. The important point to realize is that your superpowers *strengthen* you. You become more alive when you are utilizing those powers—doing them, as well as Being them.

IS IT A STRENGTH OR A SUPERPOWER?

I want to take a moment to reiterate the difference between a strength and a super-power. A strength is a skill you have a high degree of competence in. A superpower is a skill in which not only do you have a high degree of competence, but it's also something you absolutely love and enjoy doing. Your superpower makes you come alive, and it is obvious to others who are observing you in action.

Strengths and superpowers coincide from time to time, but they are not always the same thing. I've met people with perfect Scholastic Aptitude Test (SAT) scores in math, who then pursued a career in math, finance, engineering, or science, and ended up hating what they do. For some, their work was exhilarating; for others, it was a major disappointment. Some loved playing and working with numbers, and others did not. Some took a job because they had the skills and were encouraged by others. I've heard retired accountants and engineers say, "I was good at my job but never enjoyed it or found it fun." Others loved, thrived, and played all day, wedding their natural math aptitude with a job that fully used their skills and gave them a sense of fulfilling their mission.

Many people might want to offer you their opinions on what they think your mission in life should be. While many of these offerings will be well-meaning, only *you* know the difference between a strength and a superpower when it comes to *you*. Your superpower is something you are naturally, exceptionally good at. You enjoy doing it no matter how difficult or challenging the circumstances are or how it stretches you. Your superpower puts you in a zone of strength and fills you with the belief—or rather, the absolute knowing—that you can navigate whatever arises. You are energized by your superpower. And it connects you to your unique Being, genius, and purpose in life. Overall, the ripple effects of tying your strengths and superpowers together can positively impact the lives of others and the planet.

Exercise: Identify Your Superpowers

Let's take some time to identify your superpowers. Here are a few ideas to help you:

* ✻ What is something you do that you tend to receive numerous compliments for? Write down some of these compliments and let yourself truly take them in. How do they make you feel?

- ✳ What do you do that fills you with a sense of pride and the feeling of work well done and work worth doing well?
- ✳ Keep a notebook with you over the course of a week or month, and write down every situation in which you do something that is natural, fun, energizing, and remarkable.
- ✳ Work with a personal coach to help you identify your superpower. Personal coaches lead you through a very specific process that will help you uncover your unique talents. This is especially useful if you find it difficult to do it on your own.
- ✳ Check out a comprehensive personality test or profile online. The Myers-Briggs, DISC, Predictive Index, and others can provide valuable insight into your natural abilities. There are also assessments like Gallup's StrengthsFinder, which help you identify your standout strengths.

🧍 Exercise: Fill Out Your Personal Job Profile

Too often, people end up in jobs and careers they're not happy with because they don't take the time to contemplate opportunities that utilize their special gifts and talents. A Personal Job Profile (for which you will find a template in Appendix 3) will give you the opportunity to personally reflect on and write down your interests, skills, and superpowers. These are the talents and skills that equip you to carry out your mission. When people step back and take a look at their completed profile, new avenues and possibilities automatically arise. This can open exploratory pathways they may never have previously considered.

The information gleaned from a Personal Job Profile will be helpful to you as you navigate downstream and encounter tributary opportunities that act as forks or decision points along the river.

It can be helpful after you have completed a Personal Job Profile to ask a trusted parent, partner, friend, colleague, or boss if they have anything they might add. Sometimes people see things in you and observe you in certain situations or environments that can be a helpful reflection of natural strengths you may not realize you have.

Remember that, to you, your strengths and superpowers are second nature. But to others, they're truly exceptional and possibly even life-changing. It's much too easy to underestimate yourself. Knowledge of your superpowers and the awareness that there is work you were designed to do using your superpowers can be illuminating. When you harness it, that knowledge will send you forward, so you can walk toward and engage in a job that uses those skills.

EMPLOY YOUR INNER I

Accessing your inner I (which people commonly refer to as intuition) is one of the most powerful tools available to you on your journey to find the job you were born for and align your work with your life purpose. It is easy to find. It is available to all people. However, it is often overlooked as a clue or guide on our journey through life.

I have often wondered why people continue in a job they tell me they hate and that gives them a knot in their stomach every day. To me, that's a clear sign they are not meant to be in that particular situation. Other people tell me their job is so much fun they can't believe they are paid to do it.

The Greeks referred to intuition as *nous*, which is often associated with the divine intellect and the part of us that is capable of seeing and knowing truth in a deeper way. In fact, you can view the ability to connect with and act on intuition as a powerful form of self-trust and self-knowledge. Thankfully, your intuition isn't some magical supernatural power that only some people are blessed with. In fact, it isn't supernatural at all! It is your inner I, a part of you that is always with you and that you simply need a practice for attuning to.

Your inner I is a natural impulse that lives in your body and is common to absolutely every single one of us, even though we might not yet know it...or we might never have fully used it. You learn to connect with your inner I through inner body awareness.

I think of a person's inner body awareness as the language, or vehicle, of the inner I. The inner I is that part of us that helps us to understand something immediately, not through any kind of rational process but through deep attention to and awareness of our innermost Being. And inner body awareness—the felt experience of specific sensory qualities, such as effervescence, energy, and awakeness—gives us the clues we need to act on the wisdom of the inner I.

Inner body awareness can be as simple as paying attention to how you feel inside your body in different activities, environments, and situations. It can also be as mysterious as having a gut feeling, an intuition about something, or an inner knowing that something is right or not right for you.

How does our inner body awareness work, exactly? Many contemporary researchers think of it as the result of non-conscious emotional information that we access through instinctual feelings and sensations. Our body is similar to a finely tuned instrument, and it is constantly picking up vibrations and cues from the surrounding environment. Some of this information is brought into our conscious awareness, in the form of thoughts we can then translate to language. Unfortunately, we live in a world where most of our attention is devoted to what we can process in our conscious awareness, which means we have been conditioned to not pay attention to those other, harder-to-pin-down pieces of information, which might come to us in the form of a "gut" feeling, the hair on our skin standing on end, chills running down our spine, or any number of bodily sensations that might be beckoning us to pay attention!

In today's overstimulated world, there are plenty of distractions vying for our attention. We are constantly encouraged to place our attention on external things, and we are seldom taught to tune into ourselves and our inner I. When people are busy, distracted, or caught up in ruminating, they tend to not have a lot of extra energy for inner body awareness. They don't notice the knot in their stomach, the tightness in their throat, shortness of breath, or constant severe headaches that never seem to subside. They don't stop to tune into what is happening at that moment. They don't ask themselves, "Why is this happening? What does this mean?"

But when we begin to truly listen, beyond the filters and distractions of our conscious mind, we have the ability to pick up on so much! In fact, once you learn your body's language, you will discover that it's a clear, unambiguous communicator and is on the side of you having the life you want and deserve.

When you begin to listen to and really pay attention to the messages your inner I has for you, you'll find that it has all kinds of information to help you understand yourself and your place in the world. In fact, your body itself—beyond just the thoughts formulated in your mind—can be seen as a treasure house of your life experiences, memories, emotions, and desires. Your body is the sacred home of your inner I. It's a valuable tool for insight, because while the conscious brain filters out much of the information we receive, the body does not.

When we learn to decode its cues, our inner I becomes a powerful tool for our growth and our purpose in the world. For example, if you are still uncertain about your superpower, you can determine whether or not it is indeed your superpower by utilizing inner body awareness. You will feel energized, and a positive sense of well-being will permeate you when you are engaged with your superpower.

While all of us have access to our inner I, some of us are further along the path of following its wisdom than others. Some people absolutely know in their gut when something is wrong or right, without consciously having the "information" to support that feeling. Other people might have a vague sense that they don't quite know how to process. The more we tune in with patience and mindfulness, the more we learn to flex the muscle of our inner body awareness and to trust our ability to interpret what it is we are perceiving and receiving from our inner I.

Inner body awareness becomes easier to track when you become acquainted with the mind-body sensations that accompany any given experience. For example, maybe you get goosebumps when someone you are attracted to is in the room. Perhaps you feel a peacefulness in your heart when you experience sacred solitude and the opportunity to truly be with yourself.

It's important to take the time to track these mind-body sensations in a variety of situations in your life, such as:

✳ When you are doing something that fills you with joy
✳ When you are doing something that fills you with dread
✳ When you are around people you love
✳ When you are around people toward whom you're neutral
✳ When you are around people you feel uncomfortable with or who upset you
✳ When you are in an unfamiliar situation

Overall, it's always a good idea to check in with yourself multiple times a day with the simple question, "How am I feeling inside my body?" It might sound like a minor thing, but many people often have no idea how they're feeling! The trick is to consistently give yourself time and space to slow down and take stock of your internal state.

Your body is specially designed to let you know when something is wrong or off, and to assure you when you are living in a healthy and purposeful way. Inner body awareness is the feeling you get inside your body that stops you in your tracks and makes it hard to move, but it's also the sense that propels you to take a step further, or work or play joyfully for hours without any regard for time. It fuels your passion, enthusiasm, and energy so that you feel replenished and ignited by what you are doing.

Inner body awareness can be an important guide throughout this entire process of accessing the voice of your inner I and finding the job you were born for. Notice the feelings and sensations in your body when you are particularly excited and joyful, when you are engaged in something you really enjoy, that you could do for hours, and that makes you lose track of time. Everything you notice is a signal that what you are doing is something you should do more of.

Exercise: Connect to Your Inner I

Below is a three-step exercise that will help you access your inner I and connect to your mission more easily.

1. Close your eyes and take several deep breaths. Slow down both your inhalation and exhalation, and simply take time to notice how your breath fills your body. If you feel distracted or agitated, imagine that with each exhalation, you are releasing this tension; with each inhalation, you are entering into a state of deeper relaxation. Sit like this for a few minutes, allowing distracting thoughts to simply melt away as you focus on your breath. Now, do a quick body scan. Feel the quality of sensation in your hands and feet. Perhaps you notice a tingling, buzzing, heat, or something else. We all feel energy in different ways; pay attention to how it comes through for you. Then, move to your feet, legs, arms, belly, chest, heart, throat, and face. Simply scan your body for any sensations that are apparent, however subtle. Without judging, simply notice places of tightness or openness, discomfort or ease.

2. Go back to the scenario of the large playroom I mentioned early in this chapter. Picture yourself walking into that room with all its toys and activity stations. Imagine the station to which you feel most drawn. Walk over to it and pick something up. Begin to play with it. Take a moment to imagine what this is like, as realistically and with as much detail as you can. (Side note: Brain-imaging research has revealed that simply imagin-

ing something can light up the same part of your brain as experiencing it would. Imagination is an incredible tool that can't be underestimated!) Notice how you feel when you tune into your body. What are the sensations associated with doing something you love? Notice things like a sense of expansion in your heart, an undulating wave-like quality in your belly, or absolutely anything else that might be surfacing. Make a note of these sensations. Now, imagine yourself walking over to the station you're least attracted to or repelled by. Pick something up and begin to play with it. What does that feel like in your body? Take time to tune in. Notice specific sensations like a constriction in your chest or a bubbling heat in your throat. Make a note of these sensations. Feel the difference between doing something that feels good and something that doesn't.

3. Think of a specific activity in your life that you enjoy doing. Give yourself the space to do it. Pay close attention to the sensations that come up—being sure to notice sights and sounds, as well as feelings that arise in your body. Tune in to make a note of what happens when you are immersed in something you love. Congratulations! Now you have a preliminary vocabulary to help you develop inner body awareness so you can recognize the messages of your inner I.

BE MAGNIFICENTLY YOU

Part of being at home in the world and in yourself is knowing exactly who you are, what you want, and what you came here to do. Consider that you are, first and foremost, a divine human being. Your source is love, peace, wisdom, and compassion. When we forget that each of us has the capacity to bring our divine identity into our work and our mission, we miss out on truly knowing the part of ourselves that has our highest good as its utmost goal. This is the part of us that is our eternal Being.

Be open to the continual unfolding of your path and purpose on this planet. There is no one "forever" answer. On your journey to align your work with your life purpose, it is so important to focus on nurturing your strengths and superpowers, as well as cultivating your relationship to your inner I. From time to time, you may stumble upon obstacles or feel frustration, but don't let these become an excuse to get down on yourself. Use your curiosity to find the aspects of yourself that are uniquely *you*. Focus on the parts of you that are legitimately remarkable, and don't succumb to negative beliefs about your faults and imperfections. It's time to claim your birthright by fearlessly embarking on that journey inward, uncovering your gifts, and sharing them with the world.

Chapter 3

LISTEN TO WHAT IS

Calling You

> *"Let yourself be silently drawn by the strange pull*
> *of what you really love. It will not lead you astray."*
> —**Rumi**, 13th-century Persian poet and scholar

For centuries, people have been "called." A calling is the very front edge of your mission. It's the voice that summons you toward your proper work.

Noah was called to build the ark.

Moses was called to Mount Sinai, where he received the Ten Commandments.

The Buddha was called to leave his palace, so he could live an ascetic life and find a way to relieve universal suffering.

Gandhi was called to lead a nonviolent movement for independence.

Martin Luther King, Jr. was called to lead the Civil Rights Movement.

Mother Teresa was called to help India's poorest.

Nelson Mandela was called to lead a peaceful termination of apartheid.

For more than a thousand years, millions of ordinary people have been called to walk the Camino de Santiago, the famous network of pilgrim routes in Northwest Spain.

Whether your calling is humble or far-reaching, it gives you an opportunity to receive information and guidance from within. This inner source can guide you toward work that's aligned with your full Being. This intelligence has been described by scientists, physicists, philosophers, theologians, mystics, poets, and spiritual leaders in a variety of ways. Some call this source God, the higher self, or universal intelligence.

When I ask someone, "What is your passion, calling, or purpose?" they often tell me they don't know. There are many people today who do not feel like they have a calling. Their work is a means to an end: a way to support themselves and their family until they retire. They may or may not like the job, company, or type of work they're doing, but it pays the bills.

When I first discuss callings with people, they have questions:

✳ Is a calling real?
✳ Can an ordinary person have one?
✳ Do you find it, or will it find you?
✳ How will you recognize it when it comes?
✳ Do you have one calling or many?

In this chapter, we'll answer these questions. You'll also gain some guidelines on how to open yourself up to what's calling you, or what can guide you on your mission.

Some people are searching for a purpose or meaning in their work or life. Some don't believe it exists. Some feel it is a frivolous pursuit. Others have a clear purpose and enjoy what they do every day. Some just love their jobs. Many people have clarity that their purpose changes and evolves over time, and they flow with those changes from one job or profession to another over the course of their career.

For example, Oprah Winfrey progressed through a series of different jobs. She may have a core purpose to help or assist other human beings on the planet, but the way she has done that—through news broadcasting, acting, hosting a talk show, working as a magazine editor, and hosting her *Super Soul Sunday* podcast—has changed and evolved over time.

The job or career that is calling you today does not have to be a "big" role with far-reaching impact, although it very well may be. It can be whatever is aligned with your Being at this moment. It may be something that touches individuals, animals, or the planet. It may have a local, national, or global impact. It may be working as a dog walker, gardener, barista, receptionist, docent, sales clerk, hostess, poet, artist, musician, engineer, scientist, businessperson, doctor, lawyer, or any other position that feels right, good, and aligned.

Sometimes, a calling isn't immediately obvious.

I'd like to share a story with you about experiencing one of my own callings in a delightfully surprising way. In 2018, my cousin, LuAnn Nigara, called me up and invited me to be a co-author of her book. She was writing a book for interior design firm entrepreneurs and had invited subject-matter experts on certain topics to author a chapter in the book. As a leadership consultant for over 25 years, I had provided LuAnn's company, as well as other Fortune 500 companies, expertise on how to grow her business and how to hire, develop, and retain exceptional people.

When she called me, I was very busy with my life and my client work, so I told her I would think about it. I had some time to decide, because the deadline to write the chapter was a few months away. There were a number of considerations in my decision. The first was that the target audience of the book was not my client base. This was a sector I had not worked in before, and I didn't really see any immediate connections to my current business. At the same time, I liked the idea of working with LuAnn and the opportunities the book would bring for us to connect and spend more time together. We were on different coasts and hadn't gotten together very often over the years. Moreover, I liked the idea of writing a chapter in a book, which would be a new challenge that brought up a mixture of mystery, anxiety, and excitement.

A month went by. I was very busy at work and had still not decided. Other things came up, and the book chapter went off my radar. One evening, LuAnn called to tell me that I'd have to decide by tomorrow. We were getting close to the deadline for the chapter, and if I wasn't going to do it, she wanted to give someone else ample time to write the chapter. She reiterated how much she would like to have me as an author in the book, as she felt I had great wisdom to share with her target audience.

I gave it some thought. Intellectually, it still didn't make sense for me and my business, and I wasn't sure if I wanted the stress and pressure, given all my business commitments.

As I sat in a hotel room in Los Angeles pondering my decision, I felt a sensation in my body that seemed to be screaming, "Yes! Do it! Write the chapter. It doesn't need to make sense—but it is what you need to do!"

My inner I told me I had to do it.

Being a co-author in LuAnn's book brought so many wonderful things to my life that I could never have known about. First, my relationship with my cousin has dramatically deepened. We have gotten to know each other better and to develop a greater love and respect for each other. Second, I have learned a great deal from LuAnn that has strengthened me as a human being and a consultant. Her big, beautiful, honest, straight talk is exceptionally well received and respected. Her openness, compassion, and ability to relate to all people with unconditional love and reverence inspires me to no end.

Interestingly, two years and many workshops, webinars, and events later, I have now worked with over three dozen interior design firms of various sizes and have a deep knowledge and appreciation for their business and the beautiful work they bring to the world! And I keep saying yes to the work because designers are so creative, innovative, passionate, driven, sharp, open to learn and apply new things to their business, and determined to succeed.

LuAnn's second book is due out in November, and again, I have another chapter in the book. LuAnn and I are facilitating mastermind classes for interior designers who want to grow their business to $5 million and more. I have more interior design firm work than I can possibly do, and I love it! Today, I am doing things I never would have imagined had I not said yes to writing that book chapter.

A calling is not something that necessarily follows logic—but you will feel it in your body and know it is something you are meant to do. When you are fully in your calling, it will be easier to take those leaps of faith I mentioned in Chapter 1—and to trust yourself and the timing around opportunities that magically fall into your lap. You will discover that, even if you have no idea what you're signing up for, the step-by-step guidance will emerge once you're willing to embark on the adventure.

So, listen to what is calling you. Sometimes you might be called in at an inopportune time. I thought I was very busy with client work and didn't have the time to write a chapter in a book—but something compelled me to do it, anyway. If you listen to what is calling you and do it, your calling will become clearer and clearer. The next time you feel the calling, you'll recognize it and act on it.

A calling is not something you have to figure out intellectually; it is something you will just feel, especially if you've cultivated the art of inner body awareness. You can cultivate the ability to clearly recognize what is calling you. Even when it is not convenient, or it sounds difficult or scary, or it's something you have never done or never thought you would do—it will be obvious that you need to say yes!

THE FOUR-STEP PROCESS TO FINDING YOUR CALLING

How do you tune in and discover what is calling you? It involves tapping into your inner I, which we discussed in the last chapter. I want to offer you some tangible steps on using your inner I to identify your calling.

In his book, *A Gift From The Stars*, Stephen Hawkins writes: "You have to find that place in the sun where you have complete stillness, and feel perfectly balanced and content within yourself…. You have to seek peace, and harmony with the world. That won't come easy…. Your mind is like a butterfly fluttering all over the place…. I'm telling you that if you truly learn how to let go of the world, then not only the world, but the entire universe would come to you."

Hawkins talks about the importance of living in the present moment and learning to quiet your mind so you can be open to hearing your intuition. He describes animals who tread lightly and deliberately, and are aware of their surroundings: "When you see thousands of birds swooping up and down, do you see them banging into each other? They always know where they are going because they use their intuitive radar. And that is what you need to do…so you can sense and hear messages being sent through the atmosphere."

We discussed your inner I in the last chapter, but here are four specific steps you can take to work with it in gaining clearer insight and direction in finding the job you were born for.

Step 1: Sit in Stillness

Start by finding a quiet, comfortable place to sit or lie down, and close your eyes. If you are sitting on a chair, make sure your feet are firmly on the ground and your spine is straight. This is your quiet, relaxing time to focus within and get in touch with your intuition.

Take a few slow, deep, long breaths. As you exhale, feel your body relax and let go. Relax the muscles in your face, neck, shoulders, arms, fingers, stomach, torso, legs, feet, and other parts of your body that may feel tight or tense. Make a conscious choice to relax the different parts of your body until it feels like your body almost melts into the chair or ground.

You may experience a grounding feeling—a strong, stable relaxed sense of peace. Continue with slow, deep inhalations and slow, deep exhalations, until you feel your body and mind relax.

Sense the energy within your body. That energy is your inner self. You may feel your hands, fingers, or other parts of your body tingle or pulsate. Feel the aliveness of your skin as it responds to the temperature around you.

Feel your heartbeat and the pulse that travels from the heart to other parts of your body. Feel how your lungs expand and contract with each breath. Feel how there is an intelligence that is keeping your body alive without your thoughts telling it to do so.

This is the energy of your life force, the intelligence of your inner I. Be open to the experience that comes forward. Relax, let go of all thoughts and expectations, and give up effort. Allow this energy, this intelligence, to guide you on this journey.

It can be helpful to focus on your breath, paying attention to each inhalation and exhalation, and the gentle flow of oxygen flowing in and out of your nostrils. The practice of focusing on your breath keeps you present in the moment so that you are no longer thinking about the past or future.

As you relax, let go of tension in your body and thoughts in your mind; enter a clear state of peace.

At this point, ask a question about your calling and listen to what comes to you. Be patient. Allow silence. Don't think of an answer. Just focus on your breath and be open to what unfolds. Ask again and keep listening. If you don't get an answer, know the answer will come to you. It is just a matter of when and how. Don't invent an answer from the logical thoughts of your mind. This is nothing the mind needs to figure out. The answer may not come to you immediately during stillness, but it will open the door for your inner I and guidance to come through. You may receive a signal the following day, or an answer or a sign later in the week.

If you have a meditation practice that takes you to stillness, then meditate, ask the question, and wait for an answer—and know the answer will come in some form.

Step 2: Look and Listen for Signs and Signals

In your daily life, you see, read, and hear many things. A message, suggestion, or idea may come to you through an article you read, a quote you encounter on social media, a song you hear, a conversation you have with a friend, something that pops up on your computer, or a letter that arrives in the mail. Messages come to you from many different avenues, so it's a good idea to be on the lookout.

Looking and listening for signs and signals is an extension of the first step. It is part of tuning in and receiving the answer. You've probably had this experience before of getting a clear sign. Perhaps you were talking to a friend, colleague, or mentor, and suddenly things became clear for you because the other person said something that resonated. Or maybe you were walking in the park, on the beach, or in the mountains, and in the stillness of nature, you received a clear sign—like seeing a butterfly or bird at just the right moment.

Dreams and the moment when you first awaken are also important channels for signs—portals to ideas, guidance, and infinite intelligence.

Einstein's theory of relativity, Descartes' formation of the scientific method, and Mendeleev's periodic table of elements came to them through their dreams. Scientists, mathematicians, inventors, authors, poets, songwriters, composers, government leaders, athletes, and others have had dreams that guided them to great feats.

I woke up one morning a few years ago and heard, "Get up and write a book about tuning into your next job/life opportunity." I immediately went to my computer and typed the title and a brief description of each chapter. I felt strongly compelled to do so (much as I felt compelled to say yes to my cousin LuAnn when she asked me to write a chapter in her book). Prior to that morning, I'd never had an idea to write my own book.

The key to knowing if the sign, signal, or voice is right is if it *feels* right to you inside your body. You literally have an internal feeling of well-being. You can sense it. It may feel like a ball of energy or excitement stirs in the center of your belly and spreads outward throughout your body. You may have heard people say, "I'll sit with it," "That sits well with me," "It doesn't sit well with me," or "I have a bad feeling about that." They are simply tuning into their inner I.

A good way to track the signs and signals that come to you, whether through dreams or simply your daily life, is to keep a journal that you write in periodically throughout the day: perhaps once after you wake up, then in the middle of the day, and finally before you go to sleep. When you awaken, jot down any images or thoughts that immediately come to mind, including messages that may have shown up in your dreams. In the middle of the day, note anything that stood out to you—including things like articles you read, images you saw, or anything else that resonated with you on a deep level. Finally, at nighttime before bed, take stock of anything else that stood out to you during the day and captured your attention or made you come alive. You can also apply your observations directly to your interests and superpowers. Write in your journal every day to see if anything came up in relation to the profile you created in Chapter 2—or clues that gave you insight about your calling.

Sometimes an idea or message will surface multiple times before you realize it as guidance or direction. Some believe that if a concept manifests three times, it is a powerful sign to stop and pay attention. Often, the signs are all around us, but we don't always take the time to recognize them when they're knocking on our door!

Exercise: Be Guided by Your Internal GPS

Set aside 20 to 30 minutes for this exercise. This can be done inside or outside your home. I have found it optimal to do it outside at a park where there are various trails and places to explore and sit. You can also get in your car with no idea of where you are going for the next 20 to 30 minutes and let yourself be guided in the moment—by making a left here, going straight, turning right, and seeing where you end up. You can walk out your front door and do the same thing. I like to try this exercise in a variety of ways and environments. It can be fun and interesting to do this exercise in a city, too, as the people and experiences that pop up in the moment can be quite rich.

The idea of this exercise is that you will begin with no specific idea, plan, or agenda for where you want to go. Imagine that you're blindfolded and asked to walk in any direction for the duration of the exercise, except your eyes are open. You might see or hear something, or just have a feeling that you want to move in a particular direction, so you follow it. You keep following or moving in the direction that attracts you.

See where your inclinations take you. What do you observe? What experiences, signs, and insights arise? When I am in a park setting with many trails and detour paths, I am often led to more hidden places. Sometimes I see a bench or picnic table and feel inclined to sit down and just stay there a while. Many times, I will be led to see things I would have missed if I'd had a plan or destination in mind. Unusual birds emerge, deer come out of nowhere, otters swim by and pop their heads out of the water as if to say hello, snakes slither past, and hummingbirds and butterflies appear. Sometimes flies, bees, or mosquitos buzz around my ears to either bring me back to the present moment when I get lost in thoughts of the past or future, or when it is time to move to a new spot.

* * *

This exercise will help you build trust and confidence in your inner I. You will be amazed at what unfolds. Subtle signs validating your process will occur. I have seen my trust and guidance grow exponentially over time—with extraordinary results that blossom into fruitful activities, products, services, productivity, and prosperity.

Step 3: Be Open and Receptive

To be open and receptive, we need to be alert and present in the moment.

Wayne Muller writes, "Our culture invariably supposes that action and accomplishment are better than rest, that doing something—anything—is better than doing nothing. Because of our desire to succeed, to meet these ever-growing expectations, we do not rest. Because we do not rest, we lose our way. We miss the compass points that would show us where to go, we bypass the nourishment that would give us succor. We miss the quiet that would give us wisdom. We miss the joy and love born of effortless delight."

Are you so busy and mentally consumed that you're not open to receive? Do you miss the signs—or do they come and you simply don't recognize them? That is entirely possible.

Take time to rest and be silent. Being alert in the present moment is indispensable to being open to receive the signs and wisdom that abound around us. When you are present in the moment, you are not thinking about the past or worrying, planning for, and dreaming about the future. You are simply here, fully available to your inner and outer worlds.

I also encourage you to open your mind to new opportunities that may not be exactly what you originally asked for but are even more aligned with who you are and what you were born to do.

Sometimes people tell me they want a specific type of job, with a certain job title, in a specific industry. They try for that job and don't get it. Then an opportunity comes up with a different job title or in a different industry, and it feels right and good, so they take it. That job subsequently leads them to an incredible career full of success, enjoyment, and prosperity. It was not the job they originally thought they wanted, but it ended up being the one most aligned with their superpowers and their calling.

Other people get that first job they thought they wanted and enjoy it for a period of time before moving on to another opportunity they like much better, without really skipping a beat or feeling unsettled that the "dream job" they landed wasn't the end-all.

There is an openness and fluidity in this process. It is not structured, defined, and rigid. The key is to keep moving toward what feels right inside your body. Check in with your inner I. It will guide you and give you feedback.

The process of checking in will look different for everyone. Some people like to meditate; other people like to take a quiet walk; still others appreciate the process of keeping a gratitude journal. I personally love driving to the coast and parking my car so I can gaze out at the ocean. All of these are ways to train the mind so it is not hopping around like a distracted bunny from one thought or task to the next. The key is to have a quiet space to drop in and be in the moment, so you are present to any insights that arise—and so you can practice receptivity, which will serve you in all situations.

Exercise: Grow Your Ability to Receive Messages

Take at least five minutes for this exercise. You can set a timer if you like, or if you have more time available, leave it open-ended. Eventually, you can allow 20 minutes or more for this activity, as the additional time spent can be quite pleasurable and fruitful.

Either sit outside your home, or at a park, beach, hiking trail, etc., and take three slow, deep breaths. With each inhale, feel your body fill up and allow it to expand to all parts of your body; with each exhale, feel your body and mind relax into a deeper state of calm.

After your three deep breaths, focus your attention on what you observe around you. What do you see, hear, and smell? If you see a bird or animal, or hear a sound, watch and listen to it. Focus on what is happening in the present moment. If your mind wanders off to thinking about something that happened in the past or something related to the future, simply notice it and bring it back to the present moment.

Continue to do this for the duration of the exercise. When you are done, take note of thoughts, insights, and callings that popped into your head during that time. Write them down in your journal. They may offer potential pointers on your journey.

✳ ✳ ✳

As you repeat this exercise, you will notice that the amount of time you can sit and be fully in the present moment will increase. Those spaces of time when you are not thinking about the past or future enable you to open to your inner I and receive messages. Tapping into your intuition becomes easier and clearer the more you do it. In her book *Knowing…the Answers Are Within*, Shawna Allard asserts, "Think of your intuition as any other skill or muscle—the more you use it, practice it and nurture it, the bigger and stronger it will grow."

Step 4: Trust in Being

Sometimes we forget that we are human *beings*, not human doings. The process of being enables us to trust, in some place deep inside ourselves, that things will work out—that the universe is a benevolent place that wants us to step into our calling and experience a sense of deep joy, fulfillment, and purpose.

When we trust in Being (which I see as the intersection between our small human self and our vast divine self), the right things will come or manifest. It is an innate knowing that is often hidden under many layers of fear and limiting beliefs. A fear might exist around not having enough or losing what you do have. However, everyone has the capacity to trust in Being and to tap into its power.

Trust that the universe will provide for you in the same way you trust your body to facilitate each heartbeat and every breath. The same knowing that your body will carry out its vital functions throughout the day will guide you to the job that is the best match for you at this time.

A beautiful way to connect with this deep trust in Being is to practice with a simple visualization. Imagine, in your mind's eye, that you are opening a door to a special place. The tendency of the mind is to want to be in control at all times, but instead of "making it up" and allowing your thoughts to dictate what's behind the door, be receptive to what wants to come through. Don't decide in advance what the place is or what it looks like; just see yourself opening the door and trust that the environment will naturally unfold before you and manifest itself. Practice working with your inner vision in such a way that you're allowing it to reveal itself instead of "doing" something to make it happen. Show up, in full trust that you will receive the message your Being has for you.

THE CALLING THAT KEEPS ON GIVING

A calling can start small. It can be a small step you feel compelled to take. That small step can lead to another step. It may then grow and develop over time and change dimensions before it finally reveals itself as a calling.

Kathy Faller, founder and executive director of Casas de Luz, a social justice organization that builds homes for families in Mexico, attended a home build in Mexico that was sponsored by her husband's work. She enjoyed it and participated in several other home builds, along with her family, over the next few years. She was so inspired by each of the experiences she had that she began thinking about what it might be like to sponsor her own home build. Because of her interest and dedication to service over the years, she was encouraged by the Mexican builders to lead one herself.

She thought, *I don't speak Spanish, I don't know anything about construction, and I do not know my way driving around the colonias in Tijuana, Mexico. How can I do this?*

Still, something stirred inside her—a full-body yes that was encouraging her to move beyond her hesitations and expand her vision of what might be possible. Little did she know that she was developing the courage to step into her calling.

Kathy felt so drawn to this newfound purpose, and so empowered by the encouragement she received from so many of the Mexican locals, that she took up the challenge. Along the way, she received tremendous support and guidance. Twelve years later, Kathy has built over 100 homes and 3 community centers. She now builds 20 homes a year and drives to Tijuana every week by herself to deliver donations. And she now speaks Spanish. This undertaking of working full time to assist families and communities in Mexico has become her passion and her number-one calling.

A calling does not necessarily find you or fall into your lap fully formed; it can evolve and reveal itself one step at a time in the present moment.

Kathy was open, listened to her heart, asked for help (within and from others) when obstacles presented themselves, and was thoroughly guided in the process of stepping into her calling. Today, her whole Being lights up when she works with families and teams in Mexico—and even when she talks about her passion.

When you are struggling to trust in your Being, it can be helpful to go back to Step 1 and sit in stillness. When you sit still with the question or direction you are grappling with, feel inside your body for a response. You may be reassured with a thought, feeling, bodily sensation, state of inner peace, or a voice that tells you you're on track. Conversely, you may have an uncomfortable feeling that signals you are off track. If you have a knot or sick feeling in your stomach, it is telling you something. The same is true if you are experiencing headaches or confusion. They are signs for you to listen.

The more you practice tuning in, the more obvious it will be to you that it's your inner I giving you the green light versus your mind making it up. If you're getting a yes, the feeling in your body will be one of peace, joy, confidence, safety, and invigoration. It will simply feel right.

There will be times when you are called to do something and feel compelled to do it, but then it gets difficult, and your ego gets in the way and causes self-doubt. Perhaps you'll have this overall feeling that you should go forward, but fear sets in. In times like these, keep opening up to trust and keep moving forward, assured that you have the skills to carry out your mission.

There were many times during Kathy's mission when things got hard and scary in Mexico. Tijuana drug lords were warring, and continuous media accounts of murder and violence dissuaded people from going to Mexico. However, Kathy persists and continues to drive to Mexico every week to take donations and build homes and community centers, without incident.

Hundreds of thousands of people throughout the world have been listening to their inner I and Being to determine and step into their calling—and you can, too.

The practice of tuning in is essential to finding the job you were born for. I promise that the more you make a habit of moving through the four steps in this chapter, the more you will begin to receive signs and affirmation that you are on the right track. And if you are not on the right track, the simple act of slowing down, becoming attuned to yourself, and being still and present will open doors. The fears and limitations that may have held you back in the past will no longer be competition for that still, small, steady, and strong voice within.

Your calling awaits you!

Chapter 4

EXPLORE
THE INFINITE
Possibilities

"When you become comfortable with uncertainty, infinite possibilities open up in your life. Fear is no longer a dominant factor in what you do, and no longer prevents you from taking action to initiate change."
—**Eckhart Tolle**, spiritual teacher and best-selling author

There is a beautiful Taoist parable about a farmer's horse that wins a prize at a show. When a neighbor stops by to congratulate the farmer, the farmer shrugs and cryptically says, "Who really knows what's good and what's bad?"

The following day, the prize horse is stolen by thieves. When the neighbor stops by, he does so with his condolences. The farmer once again shrugs and says, "Who really knows what's good and what's bad?"

Later that week, the horse manages to make an escape from the thieves, joining a wild herd. Together, the horses make their way back to the farm. The neighbor is overjoyed at the good news. But again, the farmer says, "Who really knows what's good and what's bad?"

The next day, the farmer's son attempts to break in one of the mares that was a part of the wild herd that brought the prize horse home. The farmer's son is thrown off the mare and breaks his leg. The neighbor comes by to express his sorrow, but the farmer remains neutral, as he did on all other occasions.

The next week, the army comes through the farmer's village and conscripts soldiers for the war. They don't force the farmer's son into service, as his leg is broken. Finally, the neighbor thinks of the farmer's wise words and says to himself: "Truly, who really knows what's good or bad?"

In reflecting on the tumultuous and constantly changing current of our time, I have to ask the same question: Who really knows what's good or bad? When we're aligned with infinite possibilities, we learn to remain open to what is presenting itself to us. We don't get corralled into rigid ideas of what's good or bad; instead, we commit to broadening our horizons, engaging in intentional self-discovery, continuing to be curious, and harnessing learning opportunities that light us up with passion and pleasure. We certainly don't know where they will lead, but that's part of the fun!

As unique individuals, we each have our own way of investigating and exploring what works for us. Some people follow a very logical, rational, linear, structured, and organized path. Others' exploration may be more opportunistic or organic. They follow what is appealing or interesting in the moment. There is also a path of intuition that can guide you to discover your life's purpose or next job. I tend to believe that the best way to remain open to infinite possibilities in our work and life is by employing a combination of all these approaches: logical, organic, and intuitive.

I think of a person I know who applied for a job before the Coronavirus pandemic. He was obviously overqualified but was desperate to find any job, as he'd been unemployed for a while after being laid off from a job in graphic design and marketing. The next day, the pandemic raged across the world and the business he applied to closed for a period of time. In the process of closing, the business didn't simply shutter itself. It transformed its offerings to meet the urgency of the moment. The business had originally created artwork for hospitals and nursing homes. However, due to a major shift in priorities on a global level, they decided to create plastic shields for their customers—a product that was a major necessity for most industries at this time. In doing this, the business became even more profitable.

At this point, they decided to put out another job ad—this time, for a position that required a higher level of skills. The same man who'd applied for the entry-level job months ago applied for this job. (In the interim, he'd taken a position at a morgue in New York City—a high-stress job he was willing to do because of the direness of the situation and the increasing rise in unemployment.) This time around, his skills were perfectly matched for the job at hand. And I should know, as I was part of the selection process! Today, the business is raving about how perfect he is for the job—and he's just as happy.

When I think about this young man, I consider that all three methods—logical, organic, and intuitive—worked for him, simultaneously and synergistically. He applied for jobs and took the one he was offered because he needed to pay the rent (logical); he took an opportunity to reapply to the business when it arose, which turned out to be the right move (organic); and he followed his heart and connected with the business for which he ended up working because he knew it was the right fit even if the original role in which he was interested wasn't exactly the right fit (intuitive). Similarly, you can say that the business followed the same methods in its response to the pandemic!

Just like this young man and the business that bravely changed its business offerings, you can continue to remain curious and open despite seemingly insurmountable obstacles. This is your opportunity to open up to infinite possibilities and explore what might be available to you—without labeling any experiences (including victories and so-called obstacles) as good or bad.

Chapters 1, 2, and 3 have prepared you for an open, unbridled exploration toward your mission, a job aligned with your very Being. Now, this chapter provides examples and methods of structured, linear job exploration, combined with an intuitive, serendipitous approach that is destined to help you find the job you were born for!

Exercise: Discover Your Essence and Explore the Possibilities

For this exercise, you'll need two large pieces of 11 × 17 paper, or better yet, flipchart-size paper. You'll also need pens, markers, or any colorful medium you enjoy using.

1. On the first piece of paper, write down all your skills, talents, and superpowers. Be creative! You can use words, pictures, symbols. You can use different colors, sizes, and writing style for different skills. Be sure to re-

view your personal profile, which you completed in Chapter 2. Remember, you are taking note of your divine gifts, which you were given long before you came to this Earth. When you are finished, write down on the same piece of paper, what interests you, what you are attracted to, places you enjoy, and the types of activities you like best. This is the roadmap to fulfilling your mission, because it is often these pieces of information that will lead you to the job you were born for. Remember, enjoyment is key to understanding and fulfilling your mission!

2. Altogether, this first piece of paper contains the qualities and interests that are intrinsic to who you are, which will offer you a great deal of information about your mission.

3. Now, take a look at the first piece of paper. As you look across your skills, talents, superpowers, and interests, what ideas come to mind that could be potential jobs, careers, activities, and callings that use those skills? Notice whether any of the things you are drawn to offer opportunities to use those skills. Write those ideas down on the second piece of paper. Be playful, imaginative, make it fun.

4. The second piece of paper merges your job ideas from the first page with the places, interests, and activities. For example, from that first page, perhaps photography came up as a superpower (something your good at and enjoy). You also had "exploring national parks" on the first page as an interest or calling. So, on the second piece of paper, you might write: "Photojournalist who specializes in national parks." Keep adding ideas to this list based on what you came up with from the first piece of paper. This second piece of paper offers possibilities for how your intrinsic, authentic qualities can manifest in the world as a calling.

5. Now that you have a list, take some time to flesh out how these ideas might come to fruition. Perhaps you need extra training or work experience. Maybe there are things you can move on doing right away. Or it might be that you've identified multiple environments in which you can pursue your career idea. For example, maybe one of your main career ideas was teaching. What do you want to teach? To whom? In which

environments? Maybe there are many things you can teach, or just a few that you are generally excited to teach. Sometimes two areas overlap or intersect. For example, for someone who enjoys both teaching and writing, they might be a teacher who writes and publishes books, and gives them to students.

6. As you do this activity, keep looking at both pieces of paper to spark creative ideas about career options and specific contexts for those careers.

7. Close your eyes and tell yourself that you are open to any whispers from your inner I, source energy, or the universe. (I like to close my eyes and run my hand over the two pieces of paper to note the ideas that come to me. Sometimes, ideas just pop into my head. It is almost as if the words are energy and guide me to my next steps on the second piece of paper.)

When you are all done, hang the two pieces of paper in a place where you will see them every day. Add to them if new things come up for you. These pieces of paper can be a powerful guide for considering the possibilities that are open to you. Page 1 is your essence, which can be like a guide or roadmap that unfolds over time. Page 2 offers you greater specificity for the path you want to follow on that map. Best of all, this practice includes all three of the approaches I mentioned earlier in this chapter: logical, organic, and intuitive!

GAYLA'S STORY

Before completing the exercise I've outlined above, my daughter Gayla was not 100% certain which path or direction she should take. She had lots of interests, skills, and talents, but was unsure about what to pursue after graduating from the University of California, Berkeley, with a degree in Cognitive Science. She had been mulling over many ideas but hadn't landed on the right one yet.

Gayla told me that working on the first part of the exercise (writing down her skills, superpowers, and interests) was nice to do, and it helped her see her whole self reflected on the page. The second page of the exercise was affirming of what she had already mapped in her mind. It was helpful to clarify and put into words her options. It was also helpful to solidify the options and to recognize potential directions for what to pursue. On the second page, she was also able to recognize the overlap and synergy in the three major paths (healing, teaching, and creating) that she wrote down, and how they could all be interwoven in certain career options. For example, as a psychologist, Gayla could use creative art therapies and various holistic healing modalities like meditation, and she could also teach and write books about the field.

I posted the pages she'd created in the house so she could see them throughout the day in case they sparked ideas or she had anything to add. She asked God, the angels, and her inner I to guide her to the right next steps and path. Within a week or two of creating these pages, Gayla had a catalytic encounter with her grandfather, who had passed away ten years ago. In a lucid, meditative, dream-like state, she had a conversation with her grandfather about her path forward. They talked about how the PsyD path Gayla wanted to pursue was the right path to take based on all her talents, interests, and life experiences. That was pivotal for Gayla. She then began to explore PsyD programs. One in particular called out to her. She discovered that the Wright Institute had a First Responder program that put psychologists on the scene of major disasters and traumatic events. Amidst all of this, Gayla was having dreams at night and during the day of being next to someone in an ambulance and comforting them, while also helping them access the consciousness of source energy. Gayla recognized that there had been many recurring signs and events over the course of her entire life that had been leading her to this decision.

The exercise helped Gayla recognize that she wanted to use somatic, psychodynamic, cognitive-behavioral, expressive-arts, and contemplative techniques to help people see themselves as whole beings. "As these people learn to see themselves as whole, they can begin to see others in their community as whole, too," Gayla says. "As people accept and integrate more aspects of themselves, they will welcome more diversity in their community. Healing creates ripple effects in every direction, and I want to start making those waves, whether it be in an office with a schizophrenic client or out in the field with first responders to minimize community trauma."

DEEPEN YOUR EXPLORATION

As you've already experienced, this chapter encompasses the process of identifying opportunities that mesh with one's strengths and superpowers, as well as potential work environments, individuals, and resources that can connect a person with their ideal job.

A great way to find out whether you like a career field or job is to get some type of experience in it. Whether you volunteer or find a paid or unpaid internship, you can usually tell within a few weeks to one year if that job is for you.

After college, I moved to San Diego to find a job. I went to the University of California, San Diego, career center to explore what types of jobs existed in the organizational psychology career field. I reviewed job titles, salary ranges, and job descriptions. With that information, I had a roadmap of where to start.

I used the career center resources to tap into the alumni network and contacted alumni who were currently employed in San Diego in that career field. I talked to them about their jobs, their companies, and whether they had any job openings.

After a lot of discussions about the options available within the area of organizational psychology, I **organically** decided my goal was to become an organization development consultant. The job functions sounded interesting, the skillsets matched my strengths, there was a good deal of autonomy and flexibility, and the work had lucrative potential.

I did the **logical** thing: I identified ten successful consultants in Southern California and contacted each one to gain better insight into the field by learning about each of their career paths, qualifications, skills, and experiences. I listened carefully to their various stories to better understand the skills and experience I would need to reach my goal.

One of the ten consultants stood out to me. I had an **intuitive** sense about him: There was something special about him, and his advice resonated with me. He was very specific and detailed. He recommended I work as an employee; get promoted to a manager; obtain tangible business results in a business unit; get my master's and/or PhD; teach at local colleges at night in their professional students' undergraduate, master's, and certification programs; become president of the largest professional association in my field; and then work with a consultant who was a role model in the field, so I could learn what being an exceptional consultant looked like and how one performed.

I was floored by the trajectory he'd set out for me. While his recommendations certainly wouldn't be achieved overnight, the advice sounded straightforward and doable. I took his advice, buoyed by each and every achievement to move on to the next, and it worked out well. It ultimately led to the management consulting business I have today.

Exercise: Ask Within

The process of awakening to new possibilities isn't simply about taking action in the world. It always points us back to the still, small voice within us—the powerful voice of our inner I. You began this exploration in previous chapters, so you'll continue it here as you inquire more deeply about the environments and roles that would best suit you.

Look within for ideas, guidance, and direction. Sit in stillness and ask questions that will help you begin your exploration. You may refer to the pieces of paper you generated in the last exercise. Perhaps start with questions like these:

* What brings me joy?
* What activities do I lose track of time doing?
* What environments do I like to work in?
* What type of schedule suits me? (Do I appreciate the boundaries of the 9–5 job, or do I prefer to work on my own schedule, perhaps at odd hours or throughout the week?)
* Do I prefer to work alone or with others?
* Do I prefer single-focused tasks or dynamic, changing work?
* Where and how shall I begin my job exploration? Is there someplace to go, or someone I should speak with?

See what answers naturally pop into your head. Notice how your body feels when that answer comes to mind. If you are sensing a peacefulness and feeling of well-being, go forward and follow that direction. You may want to visualize different environments and activities you are curious about. Paint a vivid picture of what it might be like, and notice your body's response. Does it feel at ease? Open-hearted? Excited? Encouraged? Like you've found the right fit?

Remember a time that felt "just right"—whether it was playing beach volleyball on a hot summer day, writing poetry in your local café during winter's introspection, or successfully hacking your phone or computer because you knew how to make it better.

What was it about that event that felt "just right"? How did it feel in your body? Did you feel clear? Enhanced?

Now, tune into each environment, activity, and career field you are exploring. Does it sit with your Being in a similar manner?

This activity will help you narrow down the options you surfaced in the first exercise and to even add new ideas to your Page 2 list of possibilities. It will also help to make your process of discovery even more tangible, as you separate out what sounds good from what will truly make your heart sing.

USING YOUR INNER I TO FIND THE RIGHT FIT

If you're new to the process of looking inward, please be patient with yourself. Practice makes improvement, and even if sensing your body's sensations is unusual territory for you, you will learn to cue in and identify the signals that are pointing you in the right direction. Know that it can take time to develop clarity and confidence. Your intuitive muscle will grow stronger the more you act on and use it. You will begin to get answers over time, even if they don't arise in those moments of stillness you take for yourself.

LuAnn Nigara, a successful business owner for 25 years, experienced an internal stirring. It had been going on inside her for many years and came to the surface loud and clear—and it refused to be ignored.

I talked to LuAnn about her ideas, desires, talents, and calling to do something totally different. She shared, "All my life I have enjoyed speaking. Whether it was one-on-one, in groups, or with large audiences, the size of the group never fazed me. I have something to teach and share with others that will help them with their business. I am going to have a podcast, go on the speaking circuit, provide practical business advice, and motivate others. This may sound crazy, but I think I can do it and want to try."

Five years later, LuAnn has produced 700 podcast episodes, generated a waitlist of paid sponsors, published three books on *The Making of A Well-Designed Business*, and has four fan clubs. She is absolutely *loving* what she is doing. She is guided by her inner I and takes bigger, bolder steps every day.

All of this occurred because of her willingness to listen to her inner I, trust her Being, take action, and work with a logical, organic, and intuitive approach in mind. As a result, her life unfolded in synergy and serendipity, bringing her (and her fans and clients!) joy and prosperity. LuAnn and thousands of people around the world listen to their inner I, love what they do, benefit others, and prosper. In opening up to the infinite possibilities, you can do exactly this.

SURFING THE INTERNET

We are living in an exciting time that is ripe with possibility. One of the great breakthroughs of our age is the Internet, which has expanded our capacity to connect and communicate—even if we are interacting with people across the globe. For most people, it is their preferred mode of communication—whether they're connecting with an affinity group of like-minded people, participating in a professional conference, ordering a pizza, posting on social media, or seeking a job opportunity beyond their immediate geographical area. Immense quantities of information are uploaded and downloaded to the Internet on a daily basis; it has truly made the world feel a lot smaller, while it has simultaneously expanded the reach of our imaginations. The Internet is like a manifestation of our collective consciousness that has the power to take us to greater heights in our dedication to our mission and purpose.

There is a great deal of exploration that can be done on the Internet. The fun thing about the Internet is that you can Google all kinds of interests and jobs: careers with animals, careers with children, careers with plants, etc., and it will bring up related websites. As you Google areas of interest, you will see additional websites specific to your area of interest. For example, if I am drawn to, excited about, and highly interested in plants, there are websites like: *Careers with Plants: Job options, salaries, & resources*; *Top agricultural careers in plant science*; *Careers in the green industry*; *How to find a job working with plants*; as well as specific job openings, like Plant Care Specialist. It's very likely that your search will uncover hidden gems and possibilities you may never have considered—simply because you didn't know they existed!

Take your interests, skills, callings, and intuitive nudges—and Google those areas. You can identify jobs within a career field or industry. You can find salary ranges of jobs in various regions of the country. You can read job descriptions of positions and review current job postings. You can also Google questions and be directed to blogs or discussion boards that answer your questions or discuss that topic. These questions might be: *How do I find a job in computer science? What can you do with a computer-science degree? What are some cool, nontraditional jobs in neuroscience?* (When I Googled that last question, I saw postings like: "5 Cool Neuroscience Careers That Will Blow Your Mind" and "Five Fascinating Jobs in Neuroscience.")

As you are reviewing jobs and job descriptions online, notice what you are getting excited about. Some jobs may seem boring, scary, difficult, or unappealing. Others will get you excited, motivated, and energized to act. If you stop and take a moment to close your eyes and focus within your body, you might notice your belly is a little excited, your heart seems to open, and you feel a general sense of well-being. *That's it!* Follow it. Whatever you have happened upon clearly resonates with your Being.

If a definitive job or career seems to resonate, Google some job openings and review the required qualifications. Go to websites of companies you would like to explore. Look at their culture, values, vision, mission, products, services, and team. Visualize yourself in that environment and get a sense of what your daily activities might look like in the context of the organizational culture.

View current job openings and bios of employees with titles you are interested in (even if you don't fully understand what the title entails, allow your curiosity and intuition to lead you). For example, if you want to be a graphic designer, project manager, operations manager, or marketing executive, look under the About Us section of an organization's website (or something similar) and you may find pictures of employees and descriptions of what they do, along with information on their background, education, and previous work experience.

For example, if you go to Redbirdgroup.com and click on Team, you will see their team members' pictures. Click on each face and you will see their job title. Click on the person, and you have a description of what they do, as well as their experience. This information can be helpful in learning more about a position and the background and experience required. It might also inspire you to write your own aspirational bio, accompanied by a visualization that helps you stretch into the kind of mission-driven life you are already creating!

PROCEED TO THE NEXT IMPORTANT STEP: THE INFORMATIONAL INTERVIEW!

Once you have a job or career that interests you, talk to friends, extended family, alumni, and whoever you can that will share information about that job and career path. Use networking services like LinkedIn, which is a great venue for finding someone in a particular job or field with whom you can talk.

Once you have an idea for a job or career, and names of people with information or experience in that area, you will want to set up a phone call or a meeting—commonly referred to as an informational interview. Informational interviews can be extremely effective—from helping you learn about a job or career field, to helping you obtain leads or job referrals.

There are many purposes for an informational interview. One or more of the ones listed below may apply to you.

* To learn about a person in a particular job (their responsibilities, skills, and expertise), their career path to their position, and what they like about the position and company
* To learn about a particular type of job, career field, or company, and what background or experience would be needed for that job or company
* To make a positive connection with someone in the career field or company you are interested in working for, who could then refer you to potential job opportunities
* To share information about yourself, your skills, and interests; to see if they have any specific advice for you on your resume, background, and experience; and to see if they have a job available or if they know of any job opportunities that fit your background and qualifications
* To ask for a referral to someone else you could meet with in the career field or company who might be willing to discuss the field, or who has a current job opening that fits your background and experience

Informational interviews provide an opportunity to meet someone in a specific job or career field and to ask them questions about what they do, their specific career path, the state of the industry, or other related questions. Distinguished professionals enjoy these conversations and consider it giving back to others or paying it forward.

Many professionals feel they have been helped by mentors in their career and would like to help others in any way they can (I'll offer a bit more information about the power of mentorship in Chapter 5). When someone agrees to an informational interview, there is an implicit understanding that the interviewee will provide anywhere from 20 minutes to an hour of their time by phone or in person to answer your questions. I suggest that you be clear on what you want to get out of the interview and have an agenda and questions ready to guide the discussion.

An informational interview is typically an open, upbeat, informal conversation. Have fun with it, and be sure to bring your authentic interest and most pressing questions into the room.

Whether you meet an interviewee in person or via Zoom or some other videoconferencing platform, dress for the interview; bring your resume, portfolio, work samples, etc.; and have a list of questions ready to ask the interviewee. Prior to the interview, take a look at the interviewee's LinkedIn profile and company website, so you are familiar with both the company and person you are meeting with and can make appropriate links and connections during the interview. In most cases, the interviewee will look at your LinkedIn profile, so make sure it is up to date and professional. They may even look at your Facebook page, so that should be business-appropriate, as well.

Informational interviews are not just for college students or those new to the workforce. I routinely have these discussions with experienced professionals in their 30s, 40s, and 50s. They will typically ask if I am open to grabbing a cup of coffee or a drink. The conversation typically follows the same flow described above. Don't feel put off if the person says they're busy. They may only have time for a brief phone call—and if this is the case, be willing to accommodate them. Show up, be professional, and demonstrate your enthusiasm and appreciation. Pursue conversations with people you know or people to whom you've already been introduced, first. Close personal or business connections usually lead to a longer phone call or in-person meeting.

When writing down your interview questions, ask yourself what you would like to know or learn from this person. A sample informational interview format and questions are provided below. You'll want to have questions prepared, and you also want to ensure that the conversation flows naturally and unfolds organically. Take notes during the interview, so you can reference these pearls of wisdom later. You never know who will contact you six or nine months from now with an opportunity! The information you learn in the interviews will help you on your journey.

Exercise: An Outline for Your Informational Interview

Keep these tips in your mind and heart, and practice them before your informational interview. The better prepared you are, the likelier it is that you will establish a meaningful rapport with your interviewee—which could lead to all kinds of new possibilities!

1. Build rapport with the interviewee. Be warm, open, and friendly, and make a personal connection. You could ask the interviewee about something you noticed on their LinkedIn page that you have in common (e.g., you went to the same college or both worked at XYZ company), or some interesting and positive news about their company. You can also establish a personal connection through whoever referred you. "I appreciate that Barbara Smith introduced us. Barbara speaks very highly of you and mentioned [fill in the blank] about you." "I am very interested in learning more about you, your role as Controller at XYZ company, and your career path to that position."

2. Ask the interviewee about themselves: "How did you get started on this career path? Tell me about your job and responsibilities. What do you enjoy about your current position and company? What types of challenges do you encounter? What skills, background, or experience do you need to do this job? If I were interested in this type of position, what would you recommend I do to prepare for it?"

3. Share who you are, your background, experience, and interests. Show the interviewee your resume. Tell them about your short- and long-term career aspirations and goals. Tell them about the work and networking you have done in the field. Tell them about the companies you have met with or are interested in working for. Relax and be yourself. Let your internal light shine!

4. Ask the interviewee if they have any advice or suggestions for you: "What do you think of my resume? Do you have any feedback or suggestions on how I can improve my resume? Do you think I have the skills and experience to do XYZ type of job? What other types of skills or education do you suggest I pursue? What suggestions do you have for me in terms of my presentation or interviewing? Do you have any other general suggestions or advice for me?" Invite candor in this process! You will want to make sure your interviewee understands you are here to learn and integrate important tips that will enable you to grow and improve.

5. Be open to what may come up organically during the interview. The interviewee may ask you to join them at a networking function, or tell you about an upcoming conference, seminar, meetup, or softball game with other professionals. These types of events or activities could very well lead to a job or another introduction or connection in your job search. Be open and ready for them to unfold—and more importantly, say yes to the opportunities as they arise.

6. Ask the interviewee if they know other people you can talk to and if they know of any job opportunities suitable for you. You need to be delicate and assess the situation in the moment before you ask these questions, as you don't want to come across as overly eager or opportunistic, or as if you are there purely to pump them for job opportunities. You might ask: "Is there anyone you know whom you think would be helpful for me to talk to? Do you know any other professionals, like yourself, who might be open to having a conversation with me and sharing their experiences? Do you currently have any open positions or needs for someone with my background and skill set? Do you know of any organizations with openings that fit my background? Do you know anyone at XYZ organization I might be able to talk to?"

7. Close the interview. Thank the interviewee for their time and suggestions. Share that you enjoyed and appreciated meeting them and hearing about

their career, and that you wish them the best in the future. Invite the opportunity to remain in contact, and let them know that if they need anything down the line, you are here!

8. Send a thank you letter. This can be a card, letter, or an email sent out within two days. Unfortunately, in our modern age, this is a step many people often forget or take for granted—but a simple acknowledgement that lets your interviewee know how much you appreciated their taking the time to connect with you is a powerful way of making a lasting impression. Thank the interviewee for their time. Tell them how much you learned and appreciated hearing about their career path, and offer any specific iotas of insight that arose from your conversation. Express a desire to stay in touch and connect on LinkedIn.

KEEP GROWING AND INNOVATING

What are you attracted to? Are you open to the infinite possibilities? Is fear a dominant factor in your life? When you become uncomfortable with uncertainty, interesting things begin to unfold. Your mission can become even clearer.

With the Coronavirus pandemic and other unforeseen events, we are learning to grow from uncertainty. It has forced us to react quickly, and adapt to and cope with major shifts in our personal and professional lives. We now have an opportunity to rebound and innovate in ways that allow us to emerge even stronger than before. After all, throughout history, times of crisis have offered us unique conditions that help us step out of our preconceived notions and make changes more quickly and effectively than we otherwise would.

Instead of recreating a new version of "normal" or merely adapting to the world we find ourselves in, we can shape our future with intention and creativity. We can seize and create new opportunities and find new pathways to growth. The changes we are living through have generated unique challenges that need solutions. These needs have not all been fulfilled, which means they are potent opportunities to create new products, services, and protocols—opportunities to move beyond "business as usual."

Are there some creative ideas or possibilities for your own work in this new climate?

Before the Great Depression, Kirk Christiansen, the founder of the LEGO brand, used to build homes and household products. Because few people were building homes during the Depression, Christiansen started to experiment with new products: toys. First, he built these toys out of wood, and then, a new material called plastic. His was the first company to make blocks out of plastic, and it would come to create the famous binding plastic LEGO bricks. That was a huge pivot in business that rendered great rewards—and it was born from a creative inquiry that can inspire each and every one of us: "What else can I do, now that circumstances beyond my control have changed my regular business?"

Take this time to be creative and playful. Instead of allowing your ideas to be dictated by pragmatism alone, brainstorm and think outside the box—and like Christiansen, have fun while you're at it!

In your search for new possibilities, be open to what is unfamiliar, counterintuitive, and without precedent. Creativity is an iterative process, and you will see how innovation thrives when you stay open indefinitely.

I am thrilled about the open field of possibilities that is forming before all of us. Our global situation has fundamentally shifted—it won't go back to normal, and it shouldn't. It should move us forward into powerful new models for life and business.

I invite you to be one of the innovators responsible for shaping our "new normal." Let these times be a compass for your innovation. May you be one of the trendsetters who helps to transform your chosen industry for the better as you expand into infinite possibilities!

Chapter 5

ENGAGE
Earth Angels

> *"When angels visit us, we do not hear the rustle of wings,*
> *nor feel the feathery touch of the breast of a dove; but*
> *we know their presence by the love they create in our hearts."*
> —**Mary Baker Eddy**, scientist and Pulitzer Prize–winning newspaper editor

A beautiful lattice of interconnectivity, communication, and nourishment flourishes beneath the earth's surface. Botanists whimsically dub this unseen latticework the *wood-wide web*.

Trees talk to one another and pass information and resources back and forth through a network of mycorrhizal fungi. Plants use this network to communicate with one another and transfer water, carbon, nitrogen, and other nutrients and minerals to saplings and fellow plants in need. Before a tree dies or if it is sick, it sends a blast of nutrients to others in need. A tree will even communicate the danger of insect infestation.

The miraculous network of fungi connects with 90% of land plants. Scientists are just beginning to learn, talk, and write about these intricate relationships, most of which occur underground.

Earth Angels are much the same way. They live among us and provide guidance, assistance, and service inconspicuously. I have met hundreds of them and know of thousands around the world. We recognize each other with a twinkle of the eye, smile, nod, or hug. We are a world-wide web of kindness and support. Their clear purpose on the planet is to help and assist others.

I know this to be true, because I am one.

Earth Angels are people who help you out of the goodness of their heart; in fact, they want nothing in return. They have come to the planet with special knowledge, gifts, talents, and connections, and it gives them joy to help and assist others. For most of them, it is not something they are consciously aware of doing. It is part of who they are and what they do naturally. It really requires no added thought or effort—and no thanks or exchange of time, money, or favor occur.

People often question this. "Why did you go out of your way for me, spend so much time with me, and go to great lengths to help me?" Angels would say they did not do that. It just happened. They were *happy* to help. When you meet an Earth Angel, smile and know that the universe has blessed you—and listen well, as your mission might depend on it!

If you look back over your life, I am sure you can think of at least one person who helped you, supported you, and offered kindness and assistance in a selfless manner. I had many Earth Angels help me along my path—and helping others today is as natural as breathing.

On your journey to find your mission, Earth Angels encourage you to look within for answers. They refer you to serendipitous connections, people, and opportunities. They seem to know somebody who knows somebody whom you could benefit from meeting or talking to. They review resumes, share interview tips, and offer career and life counseling. But mostly, they reinforce the confidence within you that is already there. They guide you back to your Being and help you open up to the magnificent person you are.

THE EARTH ANGELS OF STAFFING AGENCIES

Unbeknownst to many seekers of the job they were born to do, staffing agencies are full of Earth Angels. Only, at staffing agencies, they are paid by employers to do what they already love doing. Often, they have a natural knack for matching people with the right job and company. They put thousands of people to work each year. They want you and the companies to be happy. They want you to be exceptional at what you do and fulfilled in your job. Those results benefit everyone involved: the employee, client company, and the staffing agency.

They will partner with you to write or improve your resume; they will teach you how to interview; they will coach you through the interview process; and they will work tirelessly to place you in a position and act as a mentor while you are in the position, all to ensure that you are effective and happy.

Express Employment Professionals is one of the largest staffing agencies in the United States, Canada, and South Africa. Founded in 1983, Express annually employs more than 566,000 people across 800 franchise locations worldwide. I have worked with Express leaders and staff over many years. I have seen firsthand that the employees exhibit a genuine love and care for helping people find work and providing assistance and hope to those they cannot place with their clients.

One applicant was living out of her car because she could not afford rent without a job. One of the Earth Angels at Express made it her top priority to find this woman a job that matched her skill set right away. Within a week, the woman had a new job—and within a month, she could afford rent. If Express can't place you in a job, they will let you know and recommend resources to help you find one.

In some offices, an extensive "folder of hope" is provided to applicants they can't assist. It provides everything from interview tips, to the names of local businesses with high-volume employment needs, to local shelters and free job search resources. At Express, when an employee is sick or going in for an operation, team members are often called into that employee's office for a moment of silence and prayer. The Express founders are extraordinarily generous to their employees and community. Thousands of dollars are donated annually to celebrate, support, and assist employees and the communities they serve. They see their business as a divine service from which many benefit.

The people I have met at the organization are connected to the vision of putting a million people to work each year, and helping employees and companies thrive. Heart and hope describe their culture and are the foundation for their success.

OTHER ENCOUNTERS WITH EARTH ANGELS

Daniel was a senior in high school and the first person in his family to ever go to college. He'd just been accepted to the University of California, Santa Cruz, and was looking for a summer job before starting college. Daniel's family members work in landscaping and housekeeping. His mother, Martha, was cleaning her client Evelyn's home and was talking with Evelyn about how her son was looking for a summer job. Evelyn got a call that day from her friend Jennifer, the VP of Human Resources of a local company, asking if her college-aged children or any of their friends were looking for a summer job. They had an opening in the customer service department and needed to fill it right away. Evelyn immediately thought of Martha's son, Daniel. Jennifer told her to send over his resume, and if it looked good, they would have him take an online assessment and then come in for an interview. Nothing was guaranteed, of course, as they were likely to receive many applications.

Daniel did not have a resume. Although he felt he didn't have any customer service experience, in fact, he had worked for his parents' landscaping company for many summers. Evelyn said she would help him put a resume together, and they would send it over that day in hopes of an interview. Evelyn had worked in recruiting and HR, so she knew how to create a professional resume. She asked Daniel questions and discovered that he did, indeed, have customer and leadership experience in a variety of areas he'd never even considered: Interacting with the landscaping clients, working as a volunteer at a soccer camp, and being captain of his soccer team all provided helpful skills for this position.

Although he felt it was a long shot, he was eager and available to interview the next day and start immediately. Jennifer reviewed his resume and set up an interview with him. Daniel had never had a formal job interview before, and Evelyn and he spent time together in preparation for the interview. They had a mock interview, and Daniel gained confidence in his natural customer service, problem-solving, and leadership skills, all of which would be highly valuable on the job.

That night, he took the online assessments and showed up first thing in the morning for the interview—which went exceptionally well. The hiring manager was impressed with Daniel's warmth, calm, and professionalism. Just what they needed in a customer service representative! He got the job, meaning he was the first person in his family to land a corporate position. Daniel did such a great job that summer that the company asked him to work every summer after that, while he was still in college. Even when the company experienced layoffs, they always called Daniel back. Daniel is so highly regarded in his workplace that he's been told they will have a position for him when he graduates college. The best part of the story is that Daniel absolutely loves his job. The company culture and colleagues are a great fit for his personality, and he's doing work that he naturally loves and at which he excels.

This is a beautiful example of an Earth Angel reaching out to help someone they knew had the natural spark and talent for the job at hand. Without Evelyn's referral and her active hand in helping Daniel to build the confidence to land the job, he may never have gotten the opportunity.

Cory, a University of California, Davis graduate with a history degree is another great example of how our Earth Angels can change the course of our lives. For 12 months after graduation, he worked full-time at Starbucks. He applied for various jobs over those 12 months on his own and did not have success landing what he considered a professional career opportunity.

Kayla, a friend of his wife's mother, had worked in business and hired hundreds of people over the years in her job. She offered to talk to Cory and see if there was anything she could do to help him. Over two months, they refined his resume, looked at job posts together, and crafted compelling cover letters, and Cory applied for various jobs. When he was called for an interview, he and Kayla would discuss how to prepare for the interview. They would do mock interviews together over the phone.

Cory landed a job at Occidental College, an environment and culture he enjoyed, and his career was off and running! Since that time, he has used the skills he learned from Kayla to apply and land other jobs that appealed to him and advanced his career. One of the most valuable things he learned from Kayla was to apply for jobs even if he didn't have all the years of experience they asked for or all the skills they desired, and to show how the skills and experience he *does* have actually match what the employers want on a fundamental level.

Today, Cory loves his job and works for the Huntington Library, a world-renowned art museum and botanical garden, as an IT Specialist. It's a seemingly unlikely path, but Cory has always loved nature, as well as working with computers to assist others in solving problems and being more efficient.

Both Daniel and Cory were fortunate in finding people who became champions and advocates of their skills and talents. Even though neither of them had a preexisting close relationship with their Earth Angels, their stories are proof positive that help pops up and reaches out in mysterious ways! All we need to do is remain receptive and grateful when our Earth Angels arrive.

METHODS FOR CONNECTING WITH YOUR EARTH ANGELS

As you continue on your journey to finding the job you were born for, please remember that the most effective approach is one that follows the three-pronged method I mentioned in Chapter 4: logical, organic, and intuitive. When you do this, you will not only find even more doors opening to you—you will discover that they lead to many Earth Angels. It is not a matter of passively waiting for the skies to open and for good fortune to come your way; you need to meet life halfway.

I promise, you will find the Earth Angels who will guide you in discovering the job you were born for. But first, let your job exploration be guided by your higher self. Tap into your spiritual core.

While you tapped into possibilities in Chapter 4 by brainstorming (although I prefer to call it heartstorming!) and asking for intuitive guidance, the process of job exploration is experiential and action-oriented. There are many job search strategies one could employ to obtain a job. You will want to use your higher self to guide you on which pragmatic job search strategies to employ.

Read through the list below and focus on what resonates with you. A few strategies will jump out and sound appealing and doable. Start there. It can be highly beneficial to pursue multiple methods at once. Different strategies are more effective for some people than others.

When you employ multiple methods and track the results, you can get a sense of what works for you. If one method is not producing fruitful results, try another method. Everyone has a different capacity to take on and manage multiple priorities. Do what is comfortable for you.

Before you begin, it is helpful to know that 80% of individuals find jobs through people they know—these can be Earth Angels who lead you to other Earth Angels! Sometimes, these may be people close to you, who know you and your talents; such people often prove to be your best advocates and can help you the most. At the same time, Earth Angels can arise in the form of people we don't know very well, but who can clearly recognize our capacity for greatness and aren't afraid to say so (just as with the examples of Daniel and Cory above)!

Start with people who know you and your work in a professional capacity. Focus on those strategies first and put the most time into them. The chart below is a list of job search strategies to employ that will surely connect you with Earth Angels. A further explanation of each of these 22 job search strategies can be found in Appendix 4.

22 JOB SEARCH STRATEGIES

Personal Connections

1. Past employers and co-worker connections
2. Family and friends
3. Referrals for informational interviews
4. Career conversations within and outside companies
5. Create a new position at your current company

Electronic Connections

6. LinkedIn: Post your profile and search for positions and companies
7. Job boards: Search and apply to jobs via forums like Indeed, Monster, and Jobing
8. Social media
9. Set up a website to showcase your expertise (interface with designers and SEO experts)
10. Send a compelling email to the CEO or executive of a company you'd like to work for

Professional Network

11. Professional organizations: job postings, meetings
12. Conferences
13. Networking opportunities: Meetups
14. Search firms and temporary agencies
15. Industry job and career fairs
16. Target specific companies

College, School Connections, and Resources

17. College professors
18. College alumni
19. Fraternity/sorority connections
20. College sports coach and teammates
21. College career center resources
22. College job fairs and on-campus interviews

All the strategies above require that you use your best judgment, emotional intelligence, intuition, and gut feelings—and determine whether they are appropriate for you, given your particular situation. Employ the approaches that sound interesting to you, that call and compel you. Go with those first and see how they work for you. Use your intuition to guide you to your mission. Ultimately, your inner self knows what direction to take. Keep asking, listening, and looking for signs that point you toward your next step on your mission, and to the people who will lead you there.

Exercise: Meet with an Earth Angel

Remember the two pieces of paper from the first exercise in Chapter 4? You'll want to refer to Page 43 for this exercise. Look over the career/environment options you listed and choose one entry that appeals to you. Now, use your **logic** to identify people in your network who could offer some powerful expertise on your chosen career opportunity and ideal environment in which to pursue it. Second, use your **intuition** to narrow that list down so that it contains only the people who feel right and good to connect with, and to whom you want to reach out. Finally, take an **organic** approach and connect with the people who are actually available for an informational interview.

THE POWER OF MULTIPLE APPROACHES

Here is an example of job search strategies that Bill, a 50-year-old technical professional decided to employ after a 30-year career with more than 10 years at his last company. After considering the job search strategies above, he decided that what resonated most with him was to:

✳ Craft an exceptionally well-done LinkedIn profile that would attract internal and external recruiters
✳ Meet with and network weekly with professionals in his field who know him and highly value and appreciate his skill set, knowledge, and experience
✳ Review the weekly Job Picks for You sent to him by LinkedIn

Bill initially believed his best prospects would come from a referral from someone he knew or a recruiter who saw his profile and valued his experience. He worked with his chosen process for seven months and received an offer from a company that came from a referral from a previous co-worker. He worked in that job for more than a year and realized it was not optimal for him, so he decided to open himself up once more to a new opportunity.

Four months later, Bill came across a description from his weekly LinkedIn Job Picks for You. He thought his background and qualifications seemed perfect for the position. He was intrigued by the job description and wanted to learn more. He checked his LinkedIn connections and asked his wife to do the same, to see if either of them knew anyone who worked at the organization. Interestingly, one of them had a direct connection with a human resources professional at the company. Of course, this didn't guarantee anything beyond the fact that someone would read Bill's resume and get back to him with feedback. At the same time, Bill knew his chances were improved by virtue of being referred by someone who already held a position within the company.

The next step was to customize the resume to fit the specific opportunity. Bill reformatted his resume from a traditional chronological resume to a functional one that outlined the core functions of the job with supporting bullet points highlighting his experience and accomplishments in those areas. This was the first time Bill had used this type of resume format in his job search process. The reason he chose this format was that the title of the job was nothing like his previous job titles, and it would not be clear to someone reading his resume that he had the specific experience needed for this job based on the various titles he'd held in the past. He submitted his new resume to the HR professional, who forwarded it to the appropriate internal recruiter responsible for filling the position. The recruiter was impressed with the breadth of Bill's experience, so he forwarded his resume to the hiring manager, and an interview was immediately scheduled.

Many synergies unfolded during the interview process. There were a number of common previous employers and colleagues who brought connection and understanding on both the applicant's and employer's side. Both parties had positive feedback about each other.

The entire process moved along smoothly and swiftly. An offer was made and accepted, and Bill felt a sense of ease, comfort, and alignment. He said, "It just seemed right and felt right…there were lots of positive signs and reinforcements along the way."

As you've seen from his story, Bill actively used a logical, organic, and intuitive approach to finding the job he was born for, and he discovered supportive Earth Angels along the way who helped him along his path—and so can you!

THE NECESSITY OF MENTORSHIP

In the process of connecting with Earth Angels, I'd be remiss not to mention the importance of mentors. A mentor is a person you respect and admire, with qualities and characteristics that inspire you to emulate them. A mentor can be anyone, from a beloved teacher or parent, to an iconic figure who has excelled in bringing humanity to a new understanding of itself. The primary criteria for choosing a good mentor are that you like and respect them, and you feel you can learn from them. Ideally, this is a mutually beneficial relationship wherein your mentor also likes and respects you, and recognizes and nurtures your potential to grow, develop, and do great things. They see your magnificence, appreciate your spark, and help you to recognize your own gifts and superpowers. They are your fan, advocate, coach, and cheerleader, and they provide you with feedback that helps you grow and develop. They also aren't afraid to tell you when you are off track, and they help you make course corrections.

Since the time I grew up and first had a coach in basketball, softball, soccer, and cheerleading, I realized there was great value in having someone close to you who knows you, believes in you, wants you to succeed, and can teach you something to help you grow and develop. After sports coaches came guidance counselors, supervisors, and managers in various jobs where I worked, as well as professors in undergraduate and graduate work, colleagues, friends, and family. It truly does take a village to help and support you along your life journey, and you'll meet many Earth Angels along the way who will fulfill this role. They guide you to look within and always answer your own questions first before they give you any advice. They help you see things you don't always see at first. They help you listen to your inner voice. They know that by helping you, they are creating a beautiful cyclical process and that you will go on to help others.

When I was working on getting my master's at the University of San Francisco in Human Resources and Organization Development, I took a strong liking to one of my instructors, Linda Shoob, who was a principal in an organization development consulting firm. She had radiant energy and a positive, upbeat attitude and approach to life, and she was also highly technically skilled in consulting processes. I asked her to be my supervisor for my master's thesis on selection systems, a topic in which she had a lot of experience and expertise. As I worked on my thesis, we got to know each other better and our relationship grew. After I graduated and started my consulting career, we stayed in touch.

Linda gave me practical tools and systems that enabled me to execute specific consulting assignments in an effective manner. She role-modeled how to utilize those tools as we engaged in consulting work together with clients, working side by side. She also helped me become comfortable with the unknown and the constant change and fluidity of working as a leadership consultant. Businesses, industries, leaders, and organizational structures are constantly changing, and your ability to confidently show up ready for anything with the skills needed to facilitate solutions and partner with your clients will ensure that you succeed.

So, how do you go about finding a good mentor? One thing to note about mentors is that you can have both formal and informal mentors. A formal mentor is someone you ask to be your mentor, and then you both agree and talk about what that means and looks like. Sometimes, however, someone you admire organically grows into or becomes your mentor in your mind and you eventually might say to them, "You are a great mentor to me." Perhaps they smile humbly or they are genuinely surprised to hear you say this. At 57, I told a dear friend of mine that she was a mentor to me, and she smiled and said, "Really? I thought you were my mentor!" We both laughed. We recognize that we mentor each other in different areas of our lives. She is a renowned international author and motivational speaker who has been my inspiration and guide on my journey to being an author and speaker—and now she knows!

A mentor can simply be someone you like and admire, and whom you are eager to learn more from. If there is already an easy and natural connection, that can be the start of a mentoring relationship. Sometimes, someone you work for or with can also become a natural mentor for you.

If you feel shy or hesitant to reach out to a potential mentor, just know this is a relationship that almost always pays off. According to the Centre for Workplace Leadership 2016, 71% of Fortune 500 companies have some kind of mentoring program, as investing in leadership capability has been demonstrated to increase performance, productivity, and innovation. Moreover, 25% of employees enrolled in a mentoring program experienced a salary grade change, compared to only 5% of workers who didn't participate. In fact, mentees are promoted five times more often than people who don't participate in a mentoring program. Retention rates are also higher for both mentees and mentors than for employees who didn't participate in a mentoring program.

I have also had many mentees over the course of my career and always encourage people to reach out and stay in touch. I love to hear about their challenges and successes on their journey, and to celebrate with them. For me, mentoring can look like anything from advising my children and my children's friends, to working with young professionals, to offering heartfelt feedback to experienced businesspeople. If you are interested in mentoring, it can be nice to think of those closest to you first. Is there someone you know could use a boost of confidence or a little guidance? Let that be where you start!

Exercise: Identify Your Mentors

For this exercise, I encourage you to look back over the course of your life and think of the people whom you admired and who expressed genuine care for and belief in you. Perhaps they offered valuable role-modeling, wisdom, advice, and encouragement.

1. Use a piece of paper to note the following: Who were these mentoring Earth Angels? How did each mentoring relationship evolve? What was your role? What was their role? They may have only been a mentor during a certain period of your life or for a very specific subject matter. Take a moment to simply feel your heart fill with gratitude for their positive influence. It can be a beautiful thing to recognize and acknowledge the gifts that emerged from these special relationships.

2. Brainstorm a list of people you currently admire, respect, or want to emulate; consider family members, friends, colleagues, supervisors, industry professionals or icons, celebrities, etc. Make your list as comprehensive as possible. Be open to the infinite possibilities.

3. Look at the list in more detail and think about who's on it more deeply. What do you know about each person? What do you like about them? What do they know and like about you? Is there potential for a friendship? Narrow your list down to one to three people you feel are possible to connect with today. Keep the others in mind for the future. Be open to inviting them into your sphere down the line.

4. Consider how you can reach out to one of those potential mentors and have a conversation. Can you connect via Zoom, a phone call, in person, etc.?

5. When you meet with your potential mentor, begin by expressing your admiration and respect for them. Tell them about you and your current situation and how you would love their input on a few things. Be prepared with a few questions you would like their advice on. See how the conversation unfolds and if it seems like the door is open for additional conversations.

6. Be proactive and continue to call and engage them. Do not be disturbed if they don't call you. I had a business colleague I highly respected and admired, and I would ask him out to lunch roughly every few months to discuss specific business questions and get his advice and perspective on client issues. It became a regular thing for years, but it was never formal. We never said we were going to have lunch together quarterly, but that's what naturally happened. We also went to a different interesting restaurant each time we met because I knew he was a foodie and really enjoyed that. At first, I would ask him out to lunch and insist on paying for his kind advice. Eventually we ended up splitting it or taking turns treating each other.

KNOW THAT THE FORCES OF GOOD ARE CONSPIRING TO HELP YOU

Even when we feel bereft or believe that help is not available to us, our capacity to remain receptive and open will always draw Earth Angels and guides into our lives. While Earth Angels might review resumes, share interview tips, and provide career and life counseling, they are primarily on our path to reinforce our existing confidence and talents, and to guide us back to ourselves and our inner knowing. They help anchor us in the tangible opportunities that are within reach, while also fostering in us a willingness to expand our thinking. Through their wisdom and belief in us, they demonstrate that we can go beyond our self-imposed limitations.

Earth Angels help us remember the magic and wonder of life, which is swimming with infinite possibilities. They are the ones who remind us of our strengths and act as mirrors for our talents and innate abilities. By more intentionally inviting in serendipitous connections, people, and opportunities, we allow ourselves to become magnets for miracles. We allow ourselves to receive the goodness and joy that life has in store for us, and we become more capable of acting as conduits for others who are seeking the same.

Chapter 6

SHOW UP
AS YOUR

> *"I will not hide my tastes or aversions. I will so trust that
> what is deep is holy, that I will do strongly before the sun
> and moon whatever only rejoices me, and the heart appoints."*
> —**Ralph Waldo Emerson**, 19th-century American poet

I recall attending a business conference back in 2002 that included a variety of big-name experts offering presentations to people across a slew of industries. At some point, during one of the presentations, a woman who appeared to be very out of place walked through the door. When it was time for the next presentation, much to everyone's surprise, she made her way to the front of the room. She was one of the presenters!

I could tell from the murmur of voices and raised eyebrows that people were taken aback. After all, this woman was definitely not dressed for a business conference. She was wearing sneakers, jeans, and a nondescript shirt. She stood in front of the room without any supporting audiovisual materials or a PowerPoint script to guide her audience through. Upon first glance, she seemed ill prepared and maybe like she wasn't taking this big-deal conference all that seriously.

However, while the first impression in the room seemed to be a unanimous *Why is* she *here?*, as she began to speak, the audience quickly became mesmerized. This woman spoke with such authority and conviction, from the very depths of her heart. It didn't feel as if she were talking to an audience of hundreds; she was effortlessly conversational, as if she were having a meaningful and intimate discussion with a friend. She was open, personable, and engaging—and what's more, she was totally stripped of the typical "expert" persona that so many presenters feel they need to assume in order to reach and impress people. Her words were poetic and beautiful, not the typical "business speak" that many of us expect at these kinds of events. As I looked around me, and as I felt the openness and relaxation in my own body, I could tell that we were all connecting with what she had to say and with the values she was embodying simply through her unpretentious way of communicating. It was almost as if she were a luminous light on that stage, radiating warmth to everyone around her and touching us at the core of who we were. The impatience and apathy I'd previously registered in the room was gone; you could have heard a pin drop as the audience absorbed this woman's words and gifts.

Sound like magic? Maybe! But in my mind, this woman revealed something better than magic: authenticity. She did not simply conform to the unspoken expectations that had been laid out for all of us at that conference; instead, she talked to us and shared the genius that lived within her. For the rest of that conference, people were gushing about how amazing she'd been—all because she'd defied expectations and taken participants into a deeper and more enriching place than they'd imagined was possible.

This is the deep power of showing up with authenticity and realness, and communicating it through your words, your energy, and your presence. Your authenticity is the unique vessel that holds your specific superpowers and skills, and that allows you to convey them in only the way *you* can.

When you show up as your authentic self, beautiful things unfold. You stand taller. You don't disguise your magnificence, or hide. You trust who you are and that who you are is sacred. You provide an example to others of what it means to stand in your poise, dignity, and uniqueness.

The feeling of being in your full authenticity is one of deep peace, clarity, and contentment. Best of all, it doesn't need to be epic (although it often can feel that way when people bring their full excellence and personality into a room!). Authenticity can be perceived in the most ordinary of moments, when people are doing their jobs with a sense of full absorption and maximum joy. Think of the moments when time flies by and you are totally engaged with your interests and skills. You are 100% aligned with your spirit and what you were born to do. Often, there's a strong sense of excitement and energy that permeates every cell of your body, opens your heart, and effortlessly spills out into the room and impacts others. Best of all, when you're fully showing up as yourself, there are residual rewards. Even after you've completed the task at hand, your body and Being might be buzzing with a heightened sense of exuberance that continues to nurture you and feed your soul.

You've probably experienced this before: When you're being your full self, you light up from within. Your radiance warms everyone around you, just like the woman who spoke at the conference.

One thing I know without a doubt is that the best way to be selected for the job you were born for is to be your whole, true self. Your strengths, superpowers, and energy are absolutely necessary to carry out this role. When you are being your Being, you are unstoppable. You are on mission.

This chapter will help you to get comfortable being yourself during the job interview process. Thorough preparation and knowledge of what to expect in an interview will make it much easier to relax and be your magnificent self. That's the goal. Show up, be yourself, shine, and get hired!

You will learn everything from how to prepare for an interview, to what to expect in an interview, to common interview questions, to tips for successful phone/video interviews, to how to ace the in-person interview. Throughout this chapter, you'll also receive techniques to relax and build your confidence so you can always show up as the best and most authentic version of you.

WHY IT PAYS TO BE YOU

Years ago, I would seldom hear people speak about the importance of being yourself when looking for a job. If anything, the emphasis was usually on making a powerful first impression that was almost entirely based on an employer's perception of you. The world has changed dramatically with respect to how people get hired, and how you can get noticed by a potential employer in a way that is favorable to you.

I see a series of small waves that keep cascading in one by one, gently breaking along the shore, offering freshness to the world and new possibilities for our entire society. The old ways of doing things are no longer sufficient. Many businesses know that in a competitive marketplace, an employee whose spirit is not being nourished and fed by the work they do is likely to find a better opportunity somewhere else. The traditional way of interviewing, where a person tells the employer what they think they wish to hear, is no longer effective. In fact, it can often backfire and make a prospective employee seem disingenuous.

Authenticity and the capacity to be totally up front about your passion, your skills, your hopes, your dreams, and your intentions to grow are all important facets of living into your mission and purpose on this planet. Today, employers want to hire people who show up using their natural strengths, in environments they enjoy, and who are aligned with the company's mission. They know that for employees to be exceptional, to thrive, and to stay, the employee needs to genuinely care about what they are doing and to feel it's a natural fit for them.

The Vice President of Human Resources of Prana Clothing, a U.S.-based global manufacturer, informed me that they only hire people who show up every day as themselves. This company is a leader in sustainable clothing, with a very specific cultural ethos: "From the fields where organic cotton and hemp are grown, to the beaches where plastic bottles are harvested, to the chemicals that need to be managed upstream, to the safety and well-being of the people assembling our clothing, there is a rich and inspiring story built into each and every piece we create."

She shared a story of when she was hiring for a critical design specialist position and had the top three candidates come in for final interviews. She reviewed the resumes, and one particular candidate stood out due to his extensive experience and expertise, which were closely related to the business. She was particularly excited to meet this candidate.

When he showed up for the interview, this candidate was very formal and reserved. He was so stiff that it was difficult to determine how he would perform on the job—or if he was even excited about the position to begin with. The VP tried to loosen him up by building rapport and letting him know he could be himself—in fact, that's what the company was looking for, as the company culture is informal, open, warm, and friendly. Still, the candidate remained stiff and formal, and he came across as plastic and unreal. In contrast, the other two candidates were more relaxed and at ease. Although they didn't have as much experience, it was clear they would fit into the company culture and work well with the team.

The most technically qualified and experienced candidate was eliminated. Perhaps he would be more comfortable in a formal environment. Or maybe he was operating under the old interview paradigm! Whatever the case, the company wished him well and hired the person they knew would thrive and contribute as much as possible in their role—and this happened to be someone who wasn't afraid to be their full self!

Be yourself. You have a purpose. You have to honor your strengths, interests, and passions in order to fully step into that purpose. When you are fully and unabashedly yourself, with all your character quirks and the things that make you uniquely you, you will find the job you were born for.

Understandably, many people feel pressure to put their best foot forward, but that should never be misconstrued as putting forward a version of you that has nothing to do with your inner truth and passions. Putting your best foot forward is about fully embracing your spirit and conveying your skills in the most transparent and expressive way possible!

Even when you do that, the goal is not always to land the job. The goal is to land the job that's *aligned with your authentic self.* By showing up as your authentic self, you can best navigate the process of assessing whether you feel aligned with the company and the job.

TIPS TO PREPARE FOR YOUR FIRST INTERVIEW

If you're one of those people who tends to get sweaty palms and a racing heart before an interview, please know you're not alone. Most people I've met report a case of pre-interview jitters. You might worry about not saying or doing the right thing to impress your interviewer, or perhaps there is concern over whether you can accurately represent all your accomplishments and skills. Or maybe you silently suffer with imposter syndrome, a pattern of negating your skills and accomplishments or believing you don't deserve the opportunities that come your way.

If that's the case, I want you to rest assured that the universe has always been conspiring to open the doors that will help you fully claim your authenticity and magnificence and to live your unique purpose. You are absolutely deserving and worthy of all the good things that come your way. Sometimes, it's a matter of faking it until you make it. There are a number of things you can do before you are invited to your first interview that will make you feel more relaxed and ready when that first invitation comes along. After all, an interview is nothing more than an invitation to explore a job opportunity at an organization. You've got this!

Pay Attention to Your Physical Presentation

An interview is a special occasion, and employers expect that you honor it. You'll want to show up looking neat (meaning you are wearing clean, well-pressed clothing) and clean (showered, hair groomed, nails clean) for this special event. If you are interested in and attracted to a more formal, conservative company and work environment (think government or financial services), a blue, black, or gray suit is ideal for men, and a suit or interview dress for women is appropriate for most interviews. If you are interested in a career in a more nontraditional or creative environment (think a tech startup or the fashion industry), attire that is more modern, stylish, colorful, or edgy may be appropriate. Always consider industry-specific attire and job-specific nuances. Keeping these general guidelines in mind, you can still embrace your uniqueness. Maybe your dapper dress is distinctive because of the design or custom tailoring. Choose to wear whatever you feel is honoring of the special occasion, and you will be guided to the job you were born for.

As a rule, even if you end up working in an environment that does not require business attire, interview clothing tends to be different from your everyday work wardrobe. The office and company might follow a casual dress code, but interviews still require a special, more formal approach.

Most employers will automatically knock you out of the interview process for not dressing appropriately. To them, it reflects your intelligence, business knowledge, and respect for them and the special occasion. If you have any doubts about appropriate interview attire, ask the interviewer or another business professional who is currently employed in the field.

Practice Answering Standard Interview Questions

Below is a list of general questions you might be asked in a standard interview. Read them over and write down your natural answer to each. Bring your full authenticity to the process. Then, review your answers with an experienced interviewer/hiring manager for feedback (anyone you know who has hired someone and would be familiar with this process—a colleague, friend, parent, neighbor, mentor, etc.). It's best to have the person ask you the questions and to then answer them. Your answers shouldn't feel scripted; you want to ensure that you feel comfortable answering the questions and that you can do so without coming across as having rehearsed them. I have found that the more times you answer these questions out loud, the easier and more natural the answers will come.

* Why are you interested in this job? This company?
* Tell me a little about yourself.

* Walk me through your background and experience and how it relates to this job.
* Why do you feel you are qualified for this position? Why do you think you are a good fit for this position and/or company?
* What are your accomplishments?
* What have you done that you are proudest of?
* What do you know about our company?
* Describe your leadership style.
* How would someone else, such as a supervisor or a colleague, describe you?
* What are your career goals or aspirations?
* What are your strengths and weaknesses?

Behavior-based interview questions are also commonly used by employers today. These questions ask you to provide a specific example of something you have done in the past. For example:

* Tell me about the last irate customer you encountered. What did you do?
* Tell me about a particularly challenging problem you encountered at work. How was the situation resolved?
* Describe a time you were given a task with very few instructions. How did you approach it?

There are many behavior-based questions on the Internet. If you're not familiar with these types of questions, you will want to become familiar with them and prepare some suitable examples from your past experience. There are no right or wrong answers to these questions, but it is ideal to have examples of on-the-job experiences that you can readily share. These answers reveal how you operate at work and will provide the interviewer with insight into how you will perform on the job.

If you are asked a behavioral question you have not heard before, relax and take your time thinking of an example. When an interviewer asks you one of these questions, they are not expecting you to come up with an answer right away. They are happy to allow silence, so you have time to think of a specific experience or examples in which you have pride because they demonstrate your passion or other qualities about yourself that you appreciate. Be ready to explain the situation, what you did specifically, and the end result.

In addition to the standard interview questions, there are also position-specific questions that relate directly to the job you will be doing. If you look at the job post or description, you will see the specific areas the employer is likely to ask you about. Sample position-specific questions can also be found on the Internet. You can even search for interview questions for a specific job and company.

Take a look at the job posting, job summary, and list of job requirements. Now, get out a piece of paper. Make a matrix of job skills or functions in the job posting on the left and your applicable skills, experience, and tangible workplace examples on the right. Be ready for your potential employer's questions by having specific examples in mind. (See the sample matrix in Appendix 5.) Have someone review your list and your resume to ensure you have the best examples and you are not missing anything. Once you have done this, you will be more relaxed and confident about your skills and ready to answer any questions.

It can also be helpful to check LinkedIn to see if you have any connections with anyone at the company with whom you are interviewing. If so, let them know you are interviewing with that company, what the role is, and who the interviewer is. They might give you a positive referral or some specific advice that can help you during the interview.

KNOW YOUR VALUES AND WHAT'S IMPORTANT TO YOU

Applicants and employers today are interested in finding a values match. When business becomes more than business and veers into a person's values and ideals, you are likelier to make a closer connection and establish a deeper rapport with your potential employer. Moreover, employers understand that employees with a strong personal connection to their company's mission and vision are likelier to stay around for the long haul and to work hard and be fully engaged in their job.

Likewise, it's important that you as an employee feel a sense of alignment with a company's values and overall ethos. Maybe you like being in environments with a great deal of company camaraderie and collaboration. Perhaps you appreciate organizations that value professional development and that groom their employees for maximum success and satisfaction. Maybe a mission and vision that focus on making the world a kinder, safer place are absolutely integral to your job satisfaction.

So, what are your values? What values are you looking for in a company? Take some time to think through these questions. Be honest. You want to show up every day in a setting and environment that is aligned with who you are. What does that look like?

Ask yourself what you are looking for in a company. Write it down.

Ask yourself what you are looking for in a job. Write it down.

What are the most important factors in considering a job opportunity? Location, pay, size of company, what they do, the position itself, the supervisor, the team of people you will work with, the culture of the organization, the future or potential of the company or industry, future job opportunities within the company, training, vacation, or other perks? What are your top five factors in order of importance?

Is there a desired or needed salary range or compensation package? Be clear about this, and be prepared for interviewers to ask you this question. Depending on your situation, it can be advantageous to say, "I am open to the salary range posted and believe you will make me an offer commensurate with my background and experience." Great standard answer!

Here is an example of one applicant's values and how they relate to her current employer. Kaitlin wanted to work for a company that was honest, ethical, professional, high quality, and that cared about their employees and customers. She interviewed with H.G. Fenton Company and found that they demonstrated those values in their daily operation. They are fair, equitable, and transparent in their compensation practice; they provide extensive employee training and development opportunities; they regularly have conversations with customers and employees; they send out surveys to gauge satisfaction and engagement and identify opportunities for improvement; and they recognize and reward quality and professionalism. H.G. Fenton Company values include:

- ✱ We do what we say we will do, and we do it well.
- ✱ We are fair-minded and honest with each other and those with whom we do business.
- ✱ We are committed to our employees' experience, professional development, success, and quality of life.
- ✱ We are committed to our customers and the quality of their experience with us.
- ✱ We continually review and improve the quality of our business practices to achieve our goals.

Both Kaitlin and the company asked questions and provided examples that illustrated living those values during the interview. It was a perfect match. Kaitlin has been there for more than 7 years and has loved every single moment of it!

WHAT TO DO AFTER SECURING THE INTERVIEW

If you've secured an interview already, congratulations! It's important to note that getting this far is a huge accomplishment, and if you're already on the shortlist, your potential employer knows you have so much to offer!

Once you have a specific interview secured with a company, the following research and preparation is recommended for you to be prepared, relaxed, and confident in the interview—so you can truly convey who you are and why you're the right person for the job.

Know the Company Inside and Out

Before walking into your interview, be sure to research the company's history, founders, mission, vision, values, and goal. This is an important step; after all, you could be spending a good portion of your time and life with them! Check to see if they have been in the news in the past one to five years. What are the ways they stand out from their competitors? What exciting things are going on in the company today that you can talk about during the interview? Check out the organization's leadership team and hiring manager, as well as their backgrounds. Do you have anything in common with them? This could be something to share and talk about to build rapport during the interview.

Know the company's products and/or services, their customers, their marketing channel(s), and their distribution channel(s). If you've had or have any personal experience with the company's product/service, or know of anyone who does, it's important to be prepared to share this, as many companies want to assess a potential candidate's familiarity with their products/services. Be familiar with who the company competes with (know its top three competitors); who has similar products/services; how the company rates or ranks compared to their competition; how the company differs from its competition; and the ways in which it displays superior performance.

You'll also want to know about the company's culture. How do they present themselves (online presence, marketing materials, etc.)? Often, their vision/mission/value statements say a lot about who they are and how they want to be seen—casual, formal, conservative, liberal, environmental, etc. Look online and ask around.

Being as familiar with the company and its culture as possible will benefit you tremendously. If possible (and applicable), experience their business first-hand. For example, if you are applying to an entertainment company (e.g., Sea World, Disneyland, a museum, a theater, etc.), visit as a guest and participate in the guest experience. This is especially important with respect to businesses that are open to the public. It will reflect positively in your interview, as employers want to hire someone who is familiar with their company, customers, products, and services. This knowledge and experience will only benefit you. It will also help you make a decision on whether you want to work for the company, or whether the job you were born for is still waiting for you to come along!

Do not forget to ask yourself whether your values and professionalism match the company's values and professionalism. Can you responsibly represent the company in a manner that is consistent with their corporate image and culture? Sometimes, you will find that if a team is laid-back, jovial, fun-loving, friendly, and outgoing, and you don't demonstrate those behaviors in the interview, you may not fit into that team culture. If the team is serious, highly professional, reserved, and conservative, they might expect the people they hire to be similar. Read about the company culture and values ahead of time to get a better sense of whether the job you're applying for is truly the job you were born for.

Prepare Questions for the Interviewer

Interviewers expect you to come to the interview prepared with questions, as this demonstrates a potential employee who is curious and proactive, as well as excited about the prospect of working at the company. Depending on the time allotted for the interview, it is appropriate to have anywhere from five to ten questions prepared in advance. Ask the most important ones first, just in case you don't have time to get to all of them.

Think about what you genuinely want to know about the job or company. (Do not ask questions about salary, benefits, and vacation until you receive an offer or are in the final stages of the interview process.)

Here are some good standard questions to ask:

* What are your goals for the department? Business unit? Company?
* What are the company's current challenges and opportunities?

✳ What are you hoping I will do or accomplish in my first six months? Year?

✳ How do you measure success in your department? What does success look like in my role?

✳ Are there any specific projects I would need to accomplish?

✳ Are there any systems or processes you would like to see improved in your department or company?

✳ How would you describe the culture of the company? Of your department?

✳ What do you like or enjoy about working here?

✳ What was it about my resume that particularly interested you?

✳ Do you feel I have the skills and qualifications to do the job?

✳ Do you have any hesitation or concerns about my skills and qualifications to perform the job?

✳ Do you see me fitting in and working well with you and your team?

✳ What are the next steps in the interview process?

✳ What is your timeline for the hiring process?

✳ When would you like someone to start?

Plan to get the interviewer's business card or contact information so you can write them a thank-you note. Remember, this is very important! Even though you came to the interview and expressed interest during the interview, they don't truly know how passionate or interested you are in the position. Employers want to hire the most qualified, passionate, positive, professional, pleasant person they can—someone who positively reflects on them and would be fun or enjoyable to work with. Never underestimate the "I like that guy/gal" factor!

IN-PERSON INTERVIEW LOGISTICS

Make sure you are comfortable with directions and have the correct address/site/facility/office location where your interview will be held. You should have your directions down and know exactly how to get there, as well as the details of your commute, well ahead of time. Then, plan to get there an hour early!

You might be thinking, *Why? That sounds crazy!*

Parking and finding the interviewer's office can sometimes add an extra half-hour or 45 minutes to your time. You never know what to expect with traffic. You might even want to do a trial run if your situation allows. You'll also want to make sure you have all the details you'll need, such as names and phone numbers of everyone you will be interviewing with. This is especially important if you encounter some unforeseen bottleneck and need to let someone know you will be late. Plan to arrive at the interviewer's office ten minutes prior to your scheduled interview.

THE COMMON INTERVIEW FORMAT

Although there is a lot of variety in the types and styles of interviews today—based on the industry, type of job, and culture of the organization—there is a basic, common, effective interview format that most organizations use. It is designed to determine if you are a match for the company and position, and whether the company is right for you. It consists of the following eight steps:

1. **Welcome and Greeting:** The interviewer will introduce him/herself and welcome you to the organization; typically, both parties will shake hands, smile, make eye contact, and say hello. Stand tall in your magnificence, and let your grip be firm and confident!

2. **Rapport-Building:** Typically, the interviewer will take the first few minutes with the candidate to engage in small talk or pleasantries. This is an opportunity for you to settle in a bit, relax, and get comfortable. It allows you your first opportunity to establish a connection and get to know each other in a more informal, personal manner before the interview gets underway.

3. **Interviewer Introduces the Interview:** Once the small talk is over, the interviewer will usually offer a brief overview of what will take place in the interview so that you are clear about the flow and expectations (e.g., when to ask questions, etc.).

4. **Interviewer Asks Candidate Easy Opener Questions:** After providing an overview, the interviewer will initiate the interview process with a few starter questions to get things going. This is an opportunity for the interviewer to obtain some basic information and also an opportunity for you to ease into the interview. Typically, these will be questions such as: *How did you hear about this position? What do you know about the company? Tell me a little about yourself. Briefly walk me through your background and experience listed on your*

resume. Why are you interested in this position and/or our company? Why do you feel you are qualified for this position?

5. **Body of the Interview:** At this point, you'll get into the meat of the interview. This is where the interview becomes far more specific. You may be asked to provide greater details about the background and expertise noted in your resume. Your interviewer might include questions that specifically pertain to the technical skills of the job; questions about performance skills (leadership, teamwork, flexibility, organization, customer service, attention to detail, problem solving, etc.); and questions to determine if you are a good fit for the organizational culture.

6. **Interviewer Provides Information about the Job and Company:** The interviewer will then go into more detail about the position, the team you'd be working with, the company, its culture, and its values.

7. **Interviewer Asks If You Have Any Questions:** Just before the interview wraps up, the interviewer will ask you what questions you have. This is where your preparation will come in handy.

8. **Interview Close:** The interviewer will wrap things up by thanking you for applying, offering next steps in the interview process, etc. With confidence, strong eye contact, and sincerity, thank your interviewer for their time and shake hands. As you leave the office, smile at whoever crosses your path, and thank everyone you met on your way in to the interview, including the receptionist.

ADDITIONAL SELECTION-PROCESS ACTIVITIES

Interviews might also include an exercise, activity, or work sample at some point during the process. It could be during your first interview, or it might be a separate step between a first and second interviews. The likelihood of this depends on the responsibilities of the job. The following are examples of this type of query:

✻ "A common problem we experience today at XYZ Company is _____. Let's brainstorm ways to approach this problem." Or: "How would you approach this problem?" You might be given a specific timeframe (e.g., "Take this assignment home and complete by next Monday" or "Complete this assignment in ten minutes on site") to process your thoughts and formulate an answer. Or you may have to respond immediately in the flow of conversation. Be ready for either scenario.

✳ Your interviewer might hand you a dry-erase marker and ask you to outline a specific process for them on a whiteboard. Or there might be a specific formula, equation, or process written on the board that they ask you to solve or explain.

✳ Your interviewer might offer you some data to review, analyze, and make recommendations on. Or you might be asked to input data into a software program to illustrate it visually.

✳ You could be asked to write a response to a customer complaint, create a job description, or draft a memorandum that announces your hire to the organization. All of this helps the interviewer assess your communication skills in a true-to-life scenario.

TIPS FOR A SUCCESSFUL PHONE OR VIDEO INTERVIEW

Today, many selection processes begin with a phone or video interview. Moreover, the time of the pandemic has necessitated an entirely new set of expectations and possibilities. It could very well be that your interviews occur entirely via phone or web conferencing. Accordingly, it is crucial to be prepared.

Being prepared for a phone or video interview is on par with being prepared for an in-person interview. Much of what is outlined in the previous sections applies to phone/video interviews, as well. While you might prefer an invitation to interview in person, discounting the importance of a phone or video interview will leave you at a disadvantage. Aside from the fact that your chosen job might entail partially or fully remote work, a phone or web interview is often your gateway to an in-person interview, so it's best to be well prepared. Here are some tips that will improve your success:

✳ **Be Room- and Equipment-Ready:** Make sure the room and equipment are 100% ready. It is important to test your audiovisual equipment the day prior to and an hour before the interview. This is a reflection of your preparedness and professionalism. Is the room quiet? Does your cell phone get good reception? Is your Internet reliable? If you are using a computer or iPad for the call, are you familiar with all the features? Does your voice sound friendly, calm, strong, and confident on the other end of the phone? If you are interviewing via Zoom, is your web camera clear and crisp? Is the lighting in your room conducive to a good interview?

✴ **Dress for Success:** Dress as you would for an in-person interview. Make sure the background behind you is pleasant and professional, not distracting.

✴ **Be Prepared:** Have your resume, list of job accomplishments, positive examples of your work, job post/description, and your list of questions for the interviewer in front of you during your interview.

✴ **Radiate Authenticity:** Because receiving nonverbal cues can be a little more tricky if you are interviewing via phone or interview, allow yourself to be a bit more expressive than perhaps you normally would during an in-person interview. Just as you would at an in-person interview, smile and be your warm, natural, authentic self. More than anything, try to relax. If you are the right person for the job and company, they will like you and you will like them. It will feel like a natural fit!

HOW TO STAND OUT

If you watch the TV show *Shark Tank*, you'll notice that some contestants come with special personalized items for each of the hosts. Some contestants go a little above and beyond, and some go *way* above and beyond. Often, the people who went to a great effort will get a sponsor on the show. The same principle applies to employee selection: Employers want to hire people who *really* want to work for them and their organization. People who exhibit eagerness and excitement, and who demonstrate that they will pour their hearts, souls, and ingenuity into the work at hand.

What can you do to demonstrate you are one of those people? How can you bring this quality to your interview process?

Of course, you'll want to use your inner knowing and common sense to determine when it is the right time to do this. Is it during the first interview, after the first interview, or at the time of the final interview?

Examples of making your mark in the interview process include:

* Handwritten, hand-delivered thank-you notes to interviewers—after all, who does that anymore? *NO ONE*! Hint, hint…And yes, dress sharply when you deliver the thank-you note. Whether you give it to the receptionist or have an opportunity to personally say hello to and thank the hiring manager, there is great value in looking your sharpest and most work-ready!
* Share a recent positive article about the company or industry; it could be a positive market comparison between competitors, or news of launching of a new product or technology.
* Make a video or something related to the company that is fun, funny, or adds value.
* Conduct a statistical or quantitative analysis of the organization that would be highly valuable and reveals your unique skills (e.g., you are going for a marketing position, so you perform a market analysis).
* After an interview, you might have additional ideas, information, or something you feel would be valuable or pertinent to the interviewer and decide to follow up with that information the next day or a few days after the interview. Whatever you offer, be creative and professional in your endeavors!

THE RIGHT JOB IS OUT THERE FOR YOU

Of course, it is fruitless to go above and beyond if you know in your heart that it isn't the right match. After an interview, you might realize that the job and company don't really appeal to you, and you don't feel you're the right fit, either.

Or perhaps you are eager to get the job after applying, only to receive a polite rejection letter. Take it in stride. It takes time, maturity, and trust to know that if you don't get a specific job, there is something else out there you were meant to do that is ultimately better for you.

My son, Trey, had a final interview with three executives for a job he was passionate about and felt highly qualified for. The day of his interview, he had to take the subway from Queens to Brooklyn, and it was raining heavily. Substantial flooding caused subway delays and closings. Despite the chaos, he arrived on time. After the interview, he called and told me about the interview—how he felt tongue-tied and was certain he didn't adequately convey his knowledge, experience, and passion.

I listened and could feel his disappointment. After our call, I sent him this email.

Hi Trey,

In this life, each of us has a mission. Your heart, soul, and intuition will guide you to yours. Trust that you have God inside of you and is on your side.

All you have to do is close your eyes, feel your feet touch the floor, and let go. Let go of thinking. Just breathe. Your Being knows how to relax into the state that connects with God and allows everything to be as it is.

Once you are there for a while, you will get the messages you need.

The messages may come from other places, too. Signs, songs, books, a random thought that pops into your head, a chance meeting with someone that says something that sparks a new direction. Trust in God; trust in your own Being.

You are an extraordinary person with unique abilities and ideas that are meant to make an impact in this world. You are doing it already (maybe not at the pace or magnitude that you would like, but it is happening). I know lots of people, families, and organizations that have been positively impacted by your presence and contribution.

As far as jobs are concerned, you will find a job that you are passionate about and enjoy. It is out there. If this job is it, you will get the job. If it isn't, something else will come up for you. Just keep being you.

Lots of love,
Mom (A HUGE fan of Trey Hahn)

You might be wondering how things went for Trey. Trey did not get the job. He ended up deciding to get his master's in Urban Planning at the University of Amsterdam. Today, he has a consulting company in Amsterdam doing what he loves, and he continues to be amazed by the clients and jobs he is getting. He often says,

"I never dreamed I would be doing work like this, in the field and type of work I am most interested in, in a country I feel so at home in!"

The reason I share this story is to illustrate that you won't get every job you go after, no matter how qualified you may be or how stellar your efforts to prepare for the interview were. There are unforeseen internal and external factors at play, as well as your individual performance that day. Having worked with human resources and hiring managers over many years, I understand there are many factors that remain invisible to most job applicants, such as the presence of internal candidates, fluctuating job requirements, hiring freezes, budget cuts, and a host of other possibilities that have nothing to do with an applicant's worth and qualifications. Take every interview as a learning experience that prepares you for the position truly aligned with your mission.

Often, as Trey experienced, while interviews may not go the way you hoped, what you might not see at the time is that there is something better and more aligned in store for you. Had Trey gotten the job for which he'd interviewed, he would never have made the joyful discoveries that continue to unfold for him in Amsterdam. Being open to infinite possibilities continues to help us keep looking for and feeling into what is actually right for us.

Rich is another example of someone who experienced a lot of doors closing in his face before the right one finally opened. A few years into his first job out of college, Rich decided to apply for positions in another part of the country to live closer to his family and broaden his career horizons. He engaged in a number of interviews over the course of two years and was understandably frustrated. He had had many phone and in-person interviews; in many cases, he would make it all the way through the process to the final interview yet not receive an offer. He felt he was a good match for all the positions, so this experience was doubly confusing and painful.

Finally, a position came along that was the crème de la crème of all the opportunities he had seen so far. The company was an industry leader, the position offered all the responsibilities and advancement opportunities he desired, the salary was the highest he'd encountered in his search, and the position was in a great location that would allow Rich to be near his family. He enjoyed the people he met in the interviews, and the values of the organization were all aligned with his own personal values. He went through the interview process and received an offer.

Today, Rich is loving his job, and in retrospect, he is so glad he did not receive offers from those other companies!

At the end of the day, you will never know why you didn't get a certain job. Accordingly, while you can use your intuition to lead you in the right direction, you have no idea what the universe has in store for you. Keep believing in yourself, exercising your skills and superpowers, and showing up as your most authentic self. If you continue doing this, I promise you will be pleasantly surprised and duly rewarded for your commitment.

Chapter 7

YOU'VE

Got This

> *"We are not human beings having a spiritual experience.*
> *We are spiritual beings having a human experience."*
> —**Pierre Teilhard de Chardin**, French Jesuit priest,
> philosopher, and paleontologist

*M*any years ago, a wide-eyed, open-hearted, talented young man graduated from college in Detroit—eager to leave his mark on the world. The young man was naturally artistic—drawn to the magic and allure of haute couture, as well as vivid colors and patterns capable of transforming any space into an environment ripe with possibilities. However, his father wasn't crazy about the prospect of his son ending up in an unreliable job in a precarious field, so he advised his son to take a practical job, working in the automotive industry. The young man conceded and did so; in fact, he worked in the automotive industry for over a decade and proved that he had the chops and skills to do his job well. The only problem? He wasn't happy. He was deeply unsatisfied and unfulfilled, and he couldn't let go of the nagging feeling that he was not doing what he was born to do.

Thankfully, the young man didn't neglect that sense of deep inner knowing. Today, Cory Damen Jenkins is a world-renowned, award-winning interior designer, with clients hailing from all over North America, Europe, and Asia. He is a powerful example of someone who decided that it was worth it to follow his passion and his calling, even if there were no guarantees as to how successful he would be, and even if there were people who declared it was too late to make such a dramatic career change.

In having the courage to make the necessary change in his life, Cory laid the foundation for his own success. Of course, it wasn't always a smoothly paved road for Cory. When I saw him speak in February 2021 at a live webinar event with LuAnn Nigara, Cory shared that he'd knocked on 779 doors after deciding to make this major career transition—and while he could have given up at any point, his deeper conviction was so much stronger than the hundreds of no's he'd received.

As I watched LuAnn and Cory talk about their experiences, I reflected on the moment: Here were two beautiful, passionate people who had previously worked in completely different jobs from the ones in which they'd ended up…the ones that had been calling to them unceasingly. Today, both of them are living and creating from their superpowers—from what I can only describe as an unbreakable connection to source energy. Both of them are doing what they were born to do. And as they learned to step into their new careers and jobs…to simply keep showing up, even in the face of discouragement and setbacks…their lives have blossomed with success, opportunities, and powerful connections and collaborations. Both of them have unleashed so much positivity and creativity in their work that not only has it brought them to the pinnacle of success—it also continues to touch, inspire, and transform the lives of those they encounter.

From my experience, people like Cory and LuAnn are not rare specimens. I have seen thousands of brave individuals all over the world who have made the vital decision to live and work in joy by stepping fully into their superpowers and being on mission in all they do. I've also had the pleasure of seeing the contrast in people's "before" and "after." Often, many of us go through a dark night of the soul when we are misaligned with our mission and purpose or when we are working at a job or company that doesn't nourish us on a deeper level. Often, this can be accompanied by the realization that we are meant for more, and we are divinely inspired to take a wild leap of faith into the unknown, which can bring up all kinds of turbulent emotions.

But every single time I have witnessed this transformation and seen people following their hearts and intuitions, I have witnessed previously closed doors magically open.

You need not be an Albert Einstein or Steve Jobs in order to access your genius and mission. Following your calling or passion, or doing what you're born to do, doesn't require rising to celebrity status or becoming a household name. It is simply about stepping into and fully claiming that which gives you joy. I've encountered this uncontainable joy in so many regular people I've met—from my cheerful, light-filled barista at Starbucks; to my gardener, whose connection to flowers and plants generates beauty for so many people; to the salespeople, corporate trainers, and business executives I work with on a daily basis. Their mere presence uplifts, energizes, and empowers others and creates a magnificent example of how we could all be living our lives.

When you are in your divinely guided purpose, you feel fully alive. You are connected to source, and you know that you have everything you need in order to thrive—even when that figurative door gets slammed in your face. You don't see this as a reason to give up; on the contrary, you are aligned with the conviction that a better door is waiting to open for you.

BEING HUMAN AND BEING DIVINE

Contrary to how most of us envision it, the body and spirit are not two split-off, separate entities. I like to think that we are all spirits wearing a temporary Earth suit and identity; in this lifetime, we get to manifest, play, create, and interact with all of nature and life in our human form. However, our appointed purposes are ultimately divine. We are here to light up the world with the radiance of our spirit, which ultimately serves to remind everyone we encounter of their own infinite potential.

In this sense, while my book is a primer on finding the job you were born for, I think we cling to a false dichotomy when we separate our work from the rest of our lives. We do not have a separate spiritual purpose that is alienated from all other aspects of our lives. There is no need to compartmentalize your divine mission in this way; in fact, your mission is something that will naturally infuse and inform every single aspect of your existence, from your relationships to your professional pursuits. In my experience, this is the kind of holistic vantage point that enables us to be genuinely happy, successful, and prosperous.

For those of you who still feel a little befuddled as to how you can live a life in which you are effortlessly welcoming the full extent of your humanity and your divinity, I want to remind you that this book is a roadmap to finding your way. It all comes back to three core principles:

1. Pay attention to your talents and skills that you enjoy doing and—you naturally excel at doing.

2. Pay attention to what interests you, feels comfortable, feels like home, and brings you a sense of enjoyment. (It is this intersection of your natural talents/aptitudes and interests that will lead you to the job you were born for!)

3. Notice when your heart opens, and you feel the energy of excitement flowing through your veins. Continue to follow the signs and cues from your body's physical reactions and whatever you encounter in your daily life. Remember, all the guidance you need lives within you—it's just a matter of recognizing the nudges from your intuition and following them.

If you allow yourself to maintain a path of following your heart and living from your innate sense of passion and purpose, I promise that you will be led to magnificent opportunities.

One of the things that gives me great joy in my own life is the work I do building houses in Mexico for communities that are besieged by poverty and violence. Every time I drive down to Mexico, which is just an hour from my home in San Diego, I feel a strong sense of excitement, joyful anticipation, and gratitude. Even when I have people advising me not to go because of the news of murders and drug cartel violence around the border, I feel called to go. And when I get down there, it is one of the most rewarding experiences I can imagine. My heart opens wide every time I am there. I am continually surrounded by remarkable, loving, inspiring Earth Angels who are dedicated to creating a livable community for the people in the area. I continue wanting to go back to work with and assist them in whatever way I can, even if that simply means showing up in a positive, happy state of mind.

I am so grateful to get to live this life every day. I've watched and known so many people from different walks of life who feel the same way. They are fired up to do the work they are doing because they know it is indisputably aligned with their gifts, strengths, passions, and purpose. In this way, no matter what the odds may seem to be, their spirits remain buoyant and positive. They know on some level that they are supported by a force more powerful than they know.

YOU ARE SUPPORTED

Some people are uncomfortable with the word *God*. It conjures up authoritative, paternalistic, judgmental images. Others are so disillusioned with religion and fallen, wayward leaders that they prefer to dismiss the whole thing. Some sense an underlying spirit, consciousness, or presence in the universe that connects us all, but they don't have a name for it. Others believe in science, intuition, or gut feelings.

It really doesn't matter what you believe or how you label it or what glasses you're wearing that color your view of source energy. The principle remains. There is some mysterious force that guides our most heartfelt visions for our lives and that seemingly governs the synchronicities and magic we experience when we are living "on purpose." The gravitational pull people feel toward the preferences they have and their clear strengths and superpowers is patently clear. You don't have to believe or buy into anything to understand this.

You are a spiritual being connected to this inexplicable source energy, like a beam emanating from the Sun. This connection enables you to relax and melt into the presence of the divine, or whatever you wish to call it. Like an ocean wave, you are supported by the greater sea as you rise, build momentum, peak, break, and dissolve back into the ocean. You are an inextricable part of the whole.

Your connection to source energy supports your continuous movement, flow, and dance with all of life. Your presence on this planet is no mistake. When you become aware of and awaken to your talents and passions, you will naturally remember that intrinsic sense of connection to the whole. You will know from the deepest place within you that you are here, living this one wild and precious life, for a reason.

Remember, Rome wasn't built in a day, and we're all coming from vastly different perspectives and life experiences. Some people I've met have known from day one that they are here for a specific purpose, and they design a life that is custom-built to suit their strengths and interests. Still other people have a sense of what they love to do, but for whatever reason, they may encounter some resistance along their path. Perhaps they haven't learned to fully trust their Being, or they have been indoctrinated with a totally contrary vision of what success looks like. Yet other people feel lost and clueless as to what they truly love and what will nourish them; for them, it could take some more soul searching to come to a place of alignment. And still others might be unwittingly living their purpose in a quiet, unassuming, and deeply serene manner—without even realizing this is what they're doing!

Wherever you are in your journey and no matter which of the aforementioned categories you fit into, I respect your individual path and what it took to get you here. There is brilliance and beauty in your story. And no matter what your life looks like now, I know without a doubt that you have the capacity to fully tap into source energy and your unique mission. Hopefully, the exercises in this book will enable you to fully claim all this for yourself!

THE ONE THING YOU MUST DO

A couple years ago, as I was getting ready for bed, I reached for the book, *A Year with Rumi*, which was lying on my nightstand. I randomly opened up to the daily reading for February 9, a poem entitled "The One Thing You Must Do."

I read it slowly. And then, I read it again.

> *There is one thing in this world which you must never forget to do.*
> *If you forget everything else and not this, there is nothing to worry about,*
> *but if you remember everything else and forget this,*
> *then you will have done nothing your whole life.*
> *It is as if a king has sent you to some country to do a task,*
> *and you perform a hundred other services, but not the one he sent you to do.*
> *So, human beings come to this world to do particular work.*
> *That work is the purpose, and each is specific to the person.*
> *If you don't do it, it's as though a knife of the finest tempering*
> *were nailed into a wall to hang things on.*
> *For a penny an iron nail could be bought to serve for that.*
> *Remember the deep root of your being, the presence of your lord.*
> *Give your life to the one who already owns your breath and your moments.*
> *If you don't, you will be like the one who takes a precious dagger*
> *and hammers it into his kitchen wall for a peg to hold his dipper gourd.*
> *You will be wasting valuable keenness and foolishly ignoring*
> *your dignity and your purpose.*

It was profound. It was also serendipitous. For a while, I'd been feeling like I was on this Earth doing hundreds of things and wondered if I was doing the one thing I must do. I decided to ask the divine, "What is the one thing I must do?"

The answer came to me, quick and clear: "Do nothing. Be joy. Hold a joyful space for others." I laughed because it was so clear. I am very much a doer. I do a lot of things all the time. But ultimately, it's not about the doing.

There is a point when you are doing a lot of things when you lose your patience, poise, and peace in the process. I was at that point. I was so busy that I was not always in joy. I had given up the joy state to get more things done. I was negatively impacting myself and others. I smiled as I thought about how I could let all those tasks go and just be joy. That brought an enormous feeling of relief. It felt like a soothing stream of water was being gently poured over my head. The sensation started at the top of my head, relieving tension, then flowed over my face and down my body. My eyes relaxed, my shoulders dropped, my stomach settled, and my arms and legs felt light and tingly. The weight was lifted, and I felt peace.

In truth, stepping into purpose isn't about finding a single task you were born to do. You don't always have to be doing; I got this message once again last year, when I found myself in a continual state of physical exhaustion. As if the world events were not enough to slow me, my body decided to help a little more and began to shut down. I started by feeling tired in the afternoon. I didn't get the message and kept trying to do the same things I'd always done to keep my energy up.

Then, I went from tired, lethargic, and exhausted to being completely unable to move my body. This rapidly culminated in the inability to think. My mind was blank. Soon, I could barely talk. Quite simply, there was nothing to say.

Now, all of this might sound strange, but it is true. I could not move, think, or talk. I was shut down by my body and Being.

It was a clear sign.

I finally recognized the sign for what it was, and I stopped. Stopped doing. Stopped moving. Stopped talking. Stopped thinking. That's when I began to listen.

What came next was nothing less than a divine revelation. It was as if divine grace had pulled back a veil and revealed the beauty, majesty, and unity of existence. I went from being in a state of chaos, to one of exhaustion, to one of ultimate bliss and harmony.

Overall, my inner guidance system during the pandemic became strong and clear. I think back to that beautiful Rumi line: *Give your life to the one who already owns your breath and your moments.*

Instead of constantly doing, I recognized that "letting go and letting God/the universe," particularly in the times during which I felt exhausted or disconnected, was my way back "home." Today, my questions and prayers are swiftly answered. I feel myself leading with love as I sense my at-oneness with nature and everything on the planet. Everything—from the trees that stop me in my tracks and draw me in, to the animals that show up and communicate with me through their profound presence—has shown me that the love of the universe is always available to us, and every single one of us can attune to it at any moment.

Today, I know that I don't have to keep "doing" or "achieving." When I am joyful and when I choose to slow down, rest, rejuvenate, and take time for myself, all my actions come from a place of joy—which generates a whole different type of contribution.

You, too, can live from this place.

Please remember that the path back to your authentic Being and purpose is as simple as recognizing your joy. Joy is a powerful indication that you're on the right track. In fact, when people are driven by inauthentic motivations, such as the desire to make more money (which is not a terrible thing in and of itself, only when it's totally divorced from your true happiness!) or to impress others, such tactics can often backfire. But your genuine joy—which you will feel on an unmistakable bodily level—will never steer you wrong.

For 25 years, I have been watching people perform in an extraordinary manner in the jobs they were born to do—joyfully using their superpowers and thriving in the midst of organizations that align with their own personal values. They have found their mission, even though that might not be the word they use for the alignment they get to experience on a daily basis.

One extraordinarily successful person I know who has won numerous awards and received a great deal of critical acclaim once told me, "I used to feel like a strange and ugly duckling, never really fitting in and knowing my place in the world. And now I feel great. I found my place and what I was born to do!" She found her way to a company and job that allows her to be her natural self—and her performance is extraordinary. People ask her how she does it, and she says, "I just show up and be myself every day." She is in a job aligned with her Being, her gifts, and her purpose. And clearly, all of this brings her great joy.

As I've mentioned throughout this book, life will present obstacles and challenges. It may take some time for you to reflect and connect to your mission. Your mission might not be singular, and instead, might iterate and evolve over time. Be open to that. Some people love horses at age five, vow to be a veterinarian, follow that path, and love it their entire life. Others may move through multiple jobs, such as recruiter, corporate training director, human resources director, and management consultant—and feel on mission in every single position. Look for the purpose that aligns with you in the present moment. Don't overthink it. Let the human part of you be practical. Employ the tools and techniques, as well as the logical, organic, and intuitive approach, that I've delineated throughout this book. Take action in the world. That is what humans do. Likewise, as a spiritual Being, take the time to be still, listen, connect, and receive the guidance you need to know and live your mission.

You have special, unique talents, abilities, and interests that will serve you and the world. You are built with your own internal compass that knows which direction works best for you. You can move in a manner that is joyful, playful, helpful, kind, and caring in the world. Listen to your inner I. Let yourself be guided to the opportunity in which you will excel and make a positive contribution and impact.

Follow the breadcrumbs. Trust yourself. You've got this. What's more, the universe has got you!

Conclusion

> *"Your vision will become clear only when you look into your heart.*
> *Who looks outside. dreams. Who looks inside, awakens."*
> —Carl Jung, Swiss psychiatrist and founder of analytical psychology

I hope that, throughout the pages of this book, your awareness of your superpowers and your unique mission on this planet has become even more pronounced and that you have felt delightfully inspired to listen to the steadfast voice of your inner I to fulfill that mission and produce extraordinary results for yourself and the people whose lives you will surely touch.

Everyone can love their job and be exceptional at it. The seven steps I have provided throughout this book are meant to align you with your life mission and help you identify your natural strengths, so you can apply those strengths in an environment that interests you and propels you forward in magical ways. Once you've accomplished all of this, then you can show up, be yourself, perform in an exceptional manner, love what you do, and spread that love to those around you!

My ultimate goal is to offer the tools that help everyone to live and work in joy. It is a win-win for individuals and for companies when the people hired for the job are truly right. Such people are naturally exceptional at what they do, and they also love it. This is the kind of love that radiates outward and has ripple effects—not just for the company but for the world. It benefits all of us to be aligned in this manner, because joy generates the kind of results that allow us to dream better and bigger. It creates new possibilities and greater synchronicities, and it allows us to align with both our human and divine selves, so we can cultivate a planet that truly serves us all.

The more you listen to yourself and take action toward what draws you in and attracts you, the greater the likelihood that you will find and secure work that nurtures your soul and allows you to utilize your talents and gifts in an extraordinary and joyful way. And, at least from my experience, to live purposefully is to live joyfully with each breath, each heartbeat, and each activity in which we choose to immerse ourselves!

My wish for you is that you will utilize the seven steps I've outlined in this book to gain a better sense of your authentic self and purpose, and to actualize that purpose in the world. Adopt a new mindset or perspective going forward—one that opens you up to new possibilities. Even if you take just a few of the concepts you learned from the book and put them into practice starting today, you will begin to see powerful changes in your life. For example, you may want to commit to the following:

* I will only move toward things I enjoy.
* I will move closer to the kind of work environment that really attracts me.
* I will use inner body awareness to connect to my inner I, so I can recognize what is calling me and take steps in that direction.
* If I get an idea and it keeps surfacing, I will explore it further.
* I will open to the possibility of living and working in joy. When new things come along or are presented to me, I will explore them with a new mindset and the right set of tools to evaluate them.

It all comes back to slowing down enough to hear the direction and guidance that are already there for you—through internal body sensations, or a mysterious compulsion that nudges you to do something that may not make sense in the moment or that even feels a little scary. Start by taking baby steps toward these things, and notice the changes that result in your life. You've got this!

"You've got this" means that whatever you take or don't take from this book is perfectly OK.

"You've got this" means that even if you follow or don't follow the steps of the roadmap, you will find your own path. You are built with your own internal compass that knows which direction works best for you. Trust yourself and listen to your inner I.

"You've got this" means there is no one right or wrong way to go about a job search.

Don't lose faith, hope, and focus after 1, 10, 20, or 50 resumes sent, interviews conducted, and rejections received—because you are not there yet, but you will be someday. And when you get there, I promise it will be rewarding and meaningful. The journey will have been worth it!

Of course, it won't always be easy and fun. There may be times when it is difficult, hard, and challenging, but you will absolutely feel and know you are in the right place doing the right thing—learning, growing, utilizing your talents, prospering, and fulfilling your purpose. And feeling both peaceful and joyful as you do it!

I know that my vision for you is well within reach and is not simply a platitude or empty promise—because all of people I have met who are loving what they do, staying in the flow, and prospering have experienced a journey with multiple paths, synchronicities, and challenges along the way. Each change and challenge brought new adventures, along with added richness, fullness, clarity, and love to their lives.

For work is nothing else but love in action. It all comes back to love.

If you have questions or if there is anything you would like support in, you can always reach out to me on my website. I would love to help and assist you. My wish is for you to use your divine gifts for a purpose that brings you joy, peace, and abundance. May you laugh, dance, and play in your work, and express the love and light that will ignite others and inspire them to do the same. And please remember that if you ever feel lost, following the seven-step roadmap will always serve to gently pull you back on track.

As Mary Oliver writes in her timeless poem "The Journey," there is only one life you can save. And by saving that one life and living your purpose, you will act as a beacon on this Earth, continuing to beam your light brightly and joyfully so as to lead others back home to their own divine mission.

"The Journey"
By Mary Oliver

One day you finally knew
what you had to do, and began,
though the voices around you
kept shouting
their bad advice—
though the whole house
began to tremble
and you felt the old tug
at your ankles.
"Mend my life!"
each voice cried.
But you didn't stop.
You knew what you had to do,
though the wind pried
with its stiff fingers
at the very foundations,
though their melancholy
was terrible.
It was already late
enough, and a wild night,
and the road full of fallen
branches and stones.
But little by little,
as you left their voices behind,
the stars began to burn
through the sheets of clouds,
and there was a new voice
which you slowly
recognized as your own,
that kept you company
as you strode deeper and deeper
into the world,
determined to do
the only thing you could do—
determined to save
the only life you could save.

Appendix 1

TECHNICAL SKILLS
INVENTORY

✳ TECHNICAL SKILL EXAMPLES: LIST YOUR SKILLS BELOW

Computer Software   MS Office, InDesign, Photoshop, Rhino, etc.

_____

_____

_____

Computer Programming   Java, C, Python, C++. JavaScript, C#, PHP, etc.

_____

_____

_____

Information Technology   Coding, communication, networks, etc.

_____

_____

_____

Big Data Analysis   Algorithms, data analytics, modeling, statistical analysis, quantitative research and reports, etc.

_____

_____

_____

Project Management   Budget and project planning, scheduling, operations, quality control, task delegation and management, etc.

_____

_____

_____

Social Media   Blogging, digital photography and media, social media platforms, web analytics

_____

_____

_____

Technical Writing   Client relations, requirement gathering, research, technical documentation

_____

_____

_____

Job-specific technical skills   Accounting, human resources, etc.

_____

_____

_____

Languages   Spoken and written

_____

_____

_____

Appendix 2

PERFORMANCE SKILLS INVENTORY

Rate Skills	Performance Skill Examples
☐ High ☐ Medium ☐ Low	**Leadership** The ability to guide or direct others toward a specific goal or end; resolves employee problems and increases employee performance and productivity
☐ High ☐ Medium ☐ Low	**Coping** The ability to maintain a calm, positive, and focused problem-solving attitude when dealing with difficult personalities, interpersonal conflict, hostility, and time demands
☐ High ☐ Medium ☐ Low	**Problem Solving** The ability to gather and analyze data, recommend solutions, and follow through on results
☐ High ☐ Medium ☐ Low	**Managing multiple priorities** The ability to simultaneously manage a number of different projects to completion; provides service for many people for multiple projects
☐ High ☐ Medium ☐ Low	**Proactive** The ability to take action and responsibility for personal and professional success and failure; influences events and achieves specific goals; originates actions and works effectively with little supervision, direction, or precedent

Rate Skills	Performance Skill Examples
❑ High ❑ Medium ❑ Low	**Self-directed/Self-reliant** The ability to work in an independent manner with little direction to accomplish goals; initiates projects; is proactive
❑ High ❑ Medium ❑ Low	**Teamwork** The ability to work cooperatively and collaboratively with others; willingly assists other team members/employees
❑ High ❑ Medium ❑ Low	**Flexibility** The ability to adapt to a variety of internal and external circumstances, as well as changing priorities
❑ High ❑ Medium ❑ Low	**Rapport Building** The ability to put people at ease and establish trust and credibility; develops good working relationships with others by being open, reliable, and consistent
❑ High ❑ Medium ❑ Low	**Organization and Planning** The ability to set priorities, create work plans, coordinate people and resources, and (re)schedule priorities; develops and streamlines organizational systems
❑ High ❑ Medium ❑ Low	**Customer Service** The ability to probe and respond to customer's needs in a polite, professional, courteous manner; anticipates customer needs
❑ High ❑ Medium ❑ Low	**Attention to Detail** The ability to pay close attention to the details of a document/project; demonstrates a thorough approach to daily tasks
❑ High ❑ Medium ❑ Low	**Decision Making** The ability to gather data from all appropriate sources and make sound judgments and decisions
❑ High ❑ Medium ❑ Low	**Patience** The ability to remain calm, focused, and diligent in detail-oriented, trying circumstances

Rate Skills	Performance Skill Examples
❑ High ❑ Medium ❑ Low	**Persuasiveness** The ability to use interpersonal skills to influence the actions and opinions of others; guides others to reach mutual objectives
❑ High ❑ Medium ❑ Low	**Persistence** The ability to continue a task and persist in spite of difficulties or obstacles
❑ High ❑ Medium ❑ Low	**Responsiveness** The ability to respond to urgent issues and items requiring immediate action

Appendix 3

PERSONAL PROFILE WORKSHEET

✻ EDUCATION

✻ CERTIFICATIONS / LICENSES

✻ TECHNICAL SKILLS

✻ PERFORMANCE SKILLS

✻ OTHER SPECIAL SKILLS/TALENTS

✻ AWARDS, HONORS, RECOGNITIONS

✳ WORK ACCOMPLISHMENTS

What have I done to make a company money, save a company money, make a company more efficient or effective, designed and implemented a new process or procedure, made a company safe or secure?

_____

_____

_____

✳ NON-WORK ACCOMPLISHMENTS

_____

_____

✳ SUPERPOWERS

_____

_____

✳ THINGS I ENJOY

Environments _____

People_____

Activities _____

Passions _____

✳ ORGANIZATION / COMPANY

Size _____

Culture _____

Industry _____

Type of Work _____

Job Title _____

Location_____

✳ TARGET COMPANIES

_____

_____

Appendix 4

22 JOB SEARCH STRATEGIES

PERSONAL CONNECTIONS

1. Past employers and co-worker connections

* Call and set up a meeting/coffee/lunch (face-to-face) with all past employers (manager, supervisor, co-workers) with whom you feel you have a positive connection. Ask them how they have been and how the organization is doing.
* Tell them about you and what you are pursuing. Show them your resume. Ask for their suggestions regarding your resume and job search. Ask them if they know anyone they suggest you talk with regarding potential job opportunities.
* Your goal is a referral to a job or an informational interview with someone in your career field. The more people you network with in your career field, the more people who can refer you to a potential job opportunity. This is where serendipity, the universe working for you, and a referral to a job all come from.
* Ask employers/co-workers/subordinates if they would be a reference when you apply for your next job. Can you check back with them as you apply to jobs in case they know someone at the company?

---

2. Family and friends

* Where do your friends and relatives work? Do those companies hire for the kinds of positions in which you are interested? If yes, ask them to refer you.

Many employers pay their employees a referral fee for referring someone into the organization. It's a win-win for you and the person who referred you.

---

3. Referrals for informational interviews

✱ Ask past employers, past co-workers, family, and friends if they have LinkedIn connections to companies you are interested in working for or companies you are applying to. A personal referral is far more valuable then applying cold online.

✱ Prepare an email to your contacts. Let them know the companies and titles of positions you are interested in. Ask them if they can refer you to anyone for an informational interview.

✱ The format and outline of informational interviews is included in Chapter 4: Explore the Infinite Possibilities.

---

4. Career conversations within and outside companies

✱ A career conversation is an open, exploratory discussion with someone regarding career opportunities within the organization.

✱ A career conversation with your current manager may focus on your desire to grow, learn new skills, take on additional responsibilities, work yourself up to high-level responsibilities, and increase your income in your career.

✱ You can also have a similar type of conversation with that person's boss or the head of the department, division, or other leaders in your current organization. It can be beneficial to let your immediate supervisor know you are planning to do that to keep them in the loop.

✱ When having a career conversation with someone in Human Resources, share how much you enjoy working for the company and believe in the mission and vision. Let them know you are interested in growing in your career and income at the company in the long term. Show them your resume and ask what ideas or suggestions they have for you in that regard.

---

5. Create a new position at current company

✱ Identify a need in the company and demonstrate qualitative benefits to the organization for having a new position in the company. Write the job description and selection criteria, and research an appropriate salary range.

✳ Present yourself and your background to fill the opening. Create a compelling presentation with research, benchmark data, and bottom-line quantifiable results. Present your proposal for this new position to your boss, bosses' boss, VP, President, and or appropriate personnel.

✳ As organizations grow and reach certain milestones, they need to add additional functions and personnel. If you have your eyes open and harbor ideas that will make a positive impact on the business, you can create your next job within your current company.

✳ For many people, it is easier to get promoted to a new higher-level position in their own company than to hope to make that jump up in a new company where they don't have a proven track record.

ELECTRONIC CONNECTIONS

6. LinkedIn—Post a profile and search for positions and companies

✳ LinkedIn can be a valuable tool in your job search as businesses, recruiters, and head hunters will use LinkedIn to search for candidates for particular jobs and then approach them directly.

✳ Set up a profile.

✳ Make sure you have a professional picture and representation on LinkedIn. The picture should be of professional quality, and you should be dressed in business attire (consider other professionals in your field and their attire on LinkedIn). The more detail you provide in the description, the better for recruiters to reach you and to show employers what you provide through quality presentation. Always have someone give you feedback on your profile; compare your profile to other people in your career field in the jobs for which you are applying.

✳ Locate jobs.

✳ You may have both internal company recruiters as well as outside recruiters proactively contact you based on your LinkedIn profile. You can search for different job titles and geographic locations. Research people and companies as needed. Initiate conversations with individuals and companies on any interesting topics related to your industry. Join LinkedIn groups related to your industry, and let people know the types of positions you are interested in. Follow specific companies and people in your industry.

7. Job Boards

✳ First, post your profile on sites such as Monster or Jobing. Then, search for job opportunities aligned with your mission. Check every day or every few days to stay on top of the latest openings. Some openings fill fast or close to new applicants once they start the interview process. Cast a wide net and look up many different job titles.

✳ Targeted cover letters are key. Customize your cover letter and resume to address the position, skills, and qualification required for the job. Communicate competence, passion, and high interest in their specific company in your cover letter.

8. Social media

✳ Most employers and recruiters are using social media to find job candidates. There is great value in having a professional social media presence a part of your job search strategy.

✳ There are many things you can do on social media to network to find a job. There are numerous websites and resources online, such as *45 things job seekers do on social media to help you make the most of social media.* People use LinkedIn, Facebook, and Twitter to network their way into a job.

✳ Initiate conversations with individuals and companies on any interesting topics related to your industry. Make sure your Facebook is private and that you do not post anything inappropriate from a conservative businessperson's perspective. You can create a positive brand through presentations of your work on your social media accounts, blog, and/or website.

✳ All public media postings reflect you and your professionalism; if you are posting family or friend pictures directed for a smaller audience, they need to be locked to that group.

9. Set up a website to showcase your expertise

✳ Your website can be about you, display your portfolio, and include other relevant articles and information you are passionate about.

---

10. Send compelling email to CEO or executive

✳ Send a compelling email to a CEO or executive that has the power to create a position for you.

✳ Many positions are created within an organization for exceptionally passionate people with special skills, knowledge, or interests. I have seen this happen for entry-level jobs as well as mid- and high-level positions. I have seen it done as a cold call and also from a referral.

✳ The following things can aid you in this process:

1. Thorough research of the company, products, services, market, and competitors

2. Targeted development of your resume, cover letter, email, and voice introduction in relation to this company and a potential position you feel you could fill

3. Having strong, compelling facts that you can make a positive impact and difference in their business. (What's in it for them? Will you make the company money, save the company money, or make the company more efficient or effective in some way? Define the benefits of hiring you)

4. Referencing a person in the organization you know or have worked with in the past

5. Strong belief and a compelling reason that you can add significant value (quantifiable is even better) to the organization

This type of approach can be particularly effective for someone who is assertive by nature and wants to be autonomous or take on a leadership role

---

PROFESSIONAL NETWORK

11. Professional organizations

✳ Find out what professional organizations are in your career field. Join a professional organization and attend their meetings. Get to know people. Volunteer to be on a task force, conference, committee, or board. See if the professional organization posts job and networking opportunities.

12. Conferences

✳ Conferences are great places to meet people in your career field and network. There are also conferences for people new to the career field or in transition. Some conferences include a place for employers to post jobs and for people to apply. It is a great opportunity to make personal connections.

13. Networking opportunities

✳ What networking opportunities exist for you? Make a list. Some will be professional or personal, or centered around hobbies and common interests. Your goal is to meet people and explore synergies, opportunities, and connections. Find them online, ask friends and colleagues which groups they attend, and check out meetups available to you. Attend meetings with interest, enthusiasm, warmth, and professionalism. Dress professionally and bring copies of your resume. Get to know people, build relationships, and make contacts. Be open and honest, and tell people what you are looking for. You may meet an Earth Angel who will connect you with someone who has an opportunity that is perfect for you.

14. Search firms and temporary agencies

✳ Search firms, recruiters, and agencies are a tremendously positive resource to help you find opportunities. When looking for a firm, make sure they are well established and credible, and that the person you will work with has a track record of success. Many firms will have you complete an online application and submit your resume, and then contact you if they have opportunities that match your needs and background. They typically will then schedule a phone interview. Treat this call as a first step in an interview process.

✳ Take this opportunity to cast a wide net exploring all different types of opportunities. You are always in control; you can go or not go to the companies and assignments they suggest. It is great to get practice interviewing and learn how to obtain offers; you can always turn them down if you don't want them. I highly recommend you go through the entire interview process to get the offer, as this will help you in the future.

✳ Many temporary jobs lead to full-time jobs. Once you are in, working for a company, and they see your talents, you have leverage when applying to that organization for a different position and also have internal referrals—a major advantage over other candidates.

15. Industry job and career fairs

✳ Career/job fairs are held in high schools, colleges, and every major city for positions and professionals at all levels. When you go to a career/job fair, always dress professionally, bring your resume, and be ready to interview on the spot if something interests you. Career/job fairs are another way to learn about various jobs, careers, and companies, as well as interview and obtain a job. Sometimes people receive an interview time or a job right on the spot.

16. Target specific companies

✳ Make a list of companies you would like to work for. Check to see if you or friends and family have LinkedIn connections. Look at their company websites for job openings and apply online. Have any connection you have write an email to Human Resources recommending you for the position, and attach your resume.

✳ Email someone in the organization (e.g., President, Director, etc.) a personal compelling message about your strong desire to work for this company and include the skills and experience you have and what you can bring to the table to benefit them; ask to meet in person or set up a call.

✳ If possible, physically check out the company; dress professionally, wander around the office, pick up literature if they have any out, talk to people if it comes up naturally, get a sense of the culture and environment, and see what you learn. If the opportunity presents itself, ask the appropriate person about the company, introduce yourself, tell them your interests, and hand them your resume.

COLLEGE CONNECTIONS AND RESOURCES

17. College professors

* Contact professors you really liked. Chances are, they liked you, too. Many students get their first internship or career job from a referral from a college professor. Professors also have contacts in business and industry, and may be able to refer you to informational interviews in your career field.

* Contact previous professors in your major/career field who like you and in whose classes you did well (B or better) first. Attend their office hours and let them know you are looking for a job; ask for their advice and counsel. Give them a copy of your resume and follow up with a thank-you email and an electronic copy of your resume. Ask if they know anyone you should specifically talk to about jobs or careers in the field. Say you are happy to have informational interviews. Ask them specifically if they know of any firms hiring right now. Ask them if they know of specific firms that hire students right out of college. Do they know anyone at the firms you are interested in working for?

18. College alumni

* Join your college alumni association and attend their monthly functions. Find out what resources are available through your alumni association. Do they have a job bank or list of alumni who are open to being contacted for informational interviews? Most alumni organizations have job postings and networking opportunities.

* Email alumni in your career field and ask if you could meet face-to-face to learn about them, their organization, and their career path. Tell them about you and what you are pursuing. Ask for their suggestions regarding your resume and job search. Ask them if they can recommend someone else you can talk with. Connect with them on LinkedIn.

19. Fraternity/sorority connections

✱ Where did your fraternity brothers or sorority sisters get their jobs? Ask them to refer you in. Where do their parents work? Can they refer you in? In many cases, you will still need to apply online for a specific position in addition to having a fraternity or sorority connection provide an internal referral for a specific position.

20. College sports coach and teammates

✱ Talk to your coach and tell them what you are looking for. Show them your resume; ask for referrals to jobs or informational interviews. Ask your teammates where they are interviewing, how they are finding leads, and whether they or their parents have any contacts in your field of interest. Remember people like to help others when they can.

21. College career center resources

✱ Go to your career center, get to know staff, and find out all possible avenues for job opportunities. Go every day for a week or two. Talk to different people when you go in. Just stop by say hello. They will think of something for you over time.

✱ Sign up for on-campus interviews. Companies conduct on-campus interviews for various positions. Ask for a referral to hiring managers who are coming in to do on-campus interviews. Ask for a list of the companies and contact people (name and email) who have interviewed college students in your major.

✱ Access your alumni database for names of people to contact and have an informational interview with.

✱ Ask if the college has:

1. A database of alumni that are willing to have informational interviews with students or graduates
2. A job website where alumni post open jobs and students/graduates can apply
3. A database of where students have gone to work after they graduated in various majors
4. Specifically, a list of companies in ___ city that have hired XYC College students or look favorably on hiring them

22. College job fairs and on-campus interviews

✳ Many colleges hold job fairs by department for specific majors. Companies come and talk about their entry-level opportunities and schedule follow-up calls and interviews. Companies all have on-campus interviews for graduating students who might be a good fit for their entry-level positions. Check into what is available in your majors and other fields that interest you. It is a great opportunity to connect with companies and experience the interview process firsthand.

IP LICENSING DIRECTOR

Job Requirements Outlined in Job Post	My Background
Ability to market technology to industrial partners	Extensive experience working with hundreds of technology companies to understand needs, address concerns, guide business decisions
State-of-the-art knowledge in subject area and broad application of principles, theories, and concepts, such as laws, regulations, and practices pertaining to the protection and management of intellectual property (IP), university technology transfer, and scientific and/or technical skills in area of expertise	Highly competent leader with engineering and business background, well versed in a wide variety of technologies and IP principles, theories, concepts, and practices
Recognized expert in specific aspect of IP/technology transfer	More than 15 years of IP licensing leadership with a world-renowned Fortune 500 technology firm
Knowledge of contracts and grants	Managed and oversaw contractual relationships with more than 400 licensees

(continued)

Job Requirements Outlined in Job Post	My Background
Ability to perform market research and business analysis, and to develop strategies for the evaluation, prosecution, marketing, commercialization, and ongoing management of IP.	Developed a wide variety of market research, business analysis, and strategies to ensure licensees complied with agreement terms, generating quarterly revenues of more than $2B
Knowledge of IP management and patenting	Working knowledge of, and experience with, the processes related to managing and ensuring compliance with an extensive international technology IP portfolio
Strong interpersonal skills and customer service; will be responsive to the needs of industry affiliates, faculty, and students	Extensive experience in customer-facing roles, building positive licensee relationships, and ensuring internal consensus across a multifaceted organization
Demonstrated record as a team player, team leader, and mentor in a diverse environment; independent self-starter with strong work ethic who can work well with others; precise attention to detail, good follow-through, and ability to close agreements	Demonstrated ability to thrive in team environments, either as a leader or contributor; actively seeks out win-win relationships; high level of attention to detail while focusing on the big picture and reaching end goals in an effective, timely fashion
Ability to plan, organize, and prioritize assignments and work independently to complete assignments, responding appropriately to competing requirements and changing priorities	Experienced at prioritizing the needs of hundreds of licensees while addressing a wide variety of internal needs and deliverables.
Experience with international business and licensing negotiations preferred	Established lasting relationships with licensees in China, Taiwan, Japan, Korea, U.S., Europe, Latin America, and other areas worldwide

Acknowledgments

Thank you to Shawna Allard, whose three-month, seemingly effortless journey writing her book *Knowing...the answers are within* encouraged me to go forward and write this book.

Susan Fowler, your deep love and enjoyment of writing and numerous books have been a role model for me and provided inspiration, information, and opened up a writer community and network.

Mark Levy, you were instrumental to encouraging me to write from a deep place of honesty, trust, and beauty. Our work together helped my writing grow and blossom. Mark's superpowers of crafting prose, speaking, and writing are streamed directly from God. I have never seen superpowers as strong and prominent as Mark's.

Thank you, Tim Ash, for providing brutally honest feedback and prompting me to strive to write something ethereal and eternal.

I have tremendous gratitude to Nirmala Nataraj for her editorial prowess and gentle, kind, loving way of bringing out the best of me and the information in the book.

Thank you to the Weaving Influence team and Tarryn Reeves for guiding me over the finish line of publication.

Many, many thanks to friends and family who provided so much encouragement, love, and support throughout this process.

Enormous love and gratitude to God/Source, who whispered in my ear to write the book, and whose breath brought words to the page, and changed my life throughout the process.

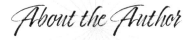

About the Author

EILEEN HAHN is an expert at hiring exceptional people, leading with love to nurture and retain staff, and helping people land the job they were born to do that brings them joy. Her work with organizational leaders for the past 25 years to hire extraordinary employees who bring fire and energy to the business, in firms like Anheuser-Busch, Ericsson Worldwide, General Motors, Pfizer, LEGOLAND, Sea World, and the San Diego Padres, has improved productivity, profitability, and employee work passion. Eileen has also studied Eastern and Western psychology, meditation, and philosophy in the U.S. and India. Her mission is for all people to live and work in joy.

Eileen received her BA in Psychology at the University of California, Santa Barbara. While there, her love of mysticism led her to double-major in Religious Studies, with a focus on the religious systems of India. Eileen went on to obtain her Master's in Human Resources and Organizational Development from the University of San Francisco—and she then carved out a career for herself in which she could blend the things she loved: business, psychology, spirituality, and helping others to become the best and most authentic versions of themselves.

Eileen has conducted thousands of interviews across industries and positions in all business sectors. She has also taught recruitment and selection, training and development, performance management, and organizational theory and behavior to undergraduate and graduate students at the University of California at San Diego, San Diego State University, and Chapman University.

Index

Made in the USA
Las Vegas, NV
28 October 2021